# THE FUTURE IS NOW

## EMERGING TRENDS IN BUSINESS

## DR. MINAKSHI BANSAL

# Dedication

*To my family, whose unwavering support and encouragement have been my foundation. To all the visionary leaders and innovators who inspire change and drive progress. And to every individual who believes in the power of responsible innovation to shape a better world.*

ppp

# Contents


*Prayer* ix

*About The Author* xi

*Preface* xv

1. The Digital Transformation - Embracing Technology For Competitive Advantage 1

**Part 1**

2. AI And Machine Learning - Revolutionizing Business Intelligence 11

**Part 2**

3. Blockchain Beyond Bitcoin - Securing Transactions And Trust 21

**Part 3**

4. The Gig Economy - Redefining The Workforce Landscape 31

**Part 4**

5. Remote Work Revolution - The Future Of The Workplace 39

**Part 5**

6. Sustainability And Green Business - Eco-Friendly Practices For Growth 49

**Part 6**

7. E-commerce Evolution - Adapting To New Consumer Behaviors 59

**Part 7**

8. Fintech Innovations - Disrupting Traditional Finance Models 69

**Part 8**

9. The Rise Of Big Data - Harnessing Information For Insight 79

**Part 9**

10. Personalization And Customer Experience - Tailoring 89

# Contents


Engagement Strategies

**Part 10**

11. Cybersecurity Imperatives - Protecting Digital Assets     99

**Part 11**

12. Smart Cities And IoT - Connecting Urban Environments     109

**Part 12**

13. The Sharing Economy - Collaborative Consumption Trends     119

**Part 13**

14. Health Tech Advances - Improving Healthcare Delivery     127

**Part 14**

15. EdTech And Online Learning - Transforming Education     137

**Part 15**

16. Virtual And Augmented Reality - Enhancing User Experiences 147

**Part 16**

17. The Future Of Retail - Blending Online And Offline Worlds     155

**Part 17**

18. Social Media Marketing - Leveraging Platforms For Brand Growth     163

**Part 18**

19. The Ethics Of Innovation - Balancing Progress With Responsibility     173

**Part 19**

20. Corporate Social Responsibility - Businesses Giving Back     183

**Part 20**

21. SUMMARY     193

Citation and References     201

# Contents


Other Books of the Author     203

CONTACT     209

# Prayer

*"Om Bhadram Karnebhih Shrinuyama Devah*

*Bhadram Pashyemakshabhiryajatrah*

*Sthirairangais Tushtuvamsastanubhih*

*Vyashema Devahitam Yadayuh*

*Svasti Na Indro Vriddhashravah*

*Svasti Nah Pusha Vishwavedah*

*Svasti Nastarkshyo Arishtanemih*

*Svasti No Brihaspatir Dadhatu*

*Om Shantih Shantih Shantih"*

*This mantra is a prayer for universal well-being, invoking the blessings of various deities for protection, health, and happiness. It emphasizes the importance of experiencing the auspicious through all senses and living a life aligned with divine purpose. The repetition of "Shantih" at the end signifies a deep desire for peace in the individual, the environment, and the universe at large. This mantra is often recited as a prayer for peace, prosperity, and the physical and spiritual well-being of all beings.*

ᐅᐅᐅ

# About The Author

This book represents the culmination of extensive research and meticulous analysis, incorporating a diverse range of sources, including numerous books, scholarly studies, and personal experiences. Additionally, I have scoured various websites to gather relevant information and data essential for the compilation of this work. I have taken every precaution to ensure the accuracy of the information presented and have diligently cited all sources to acknowledge their contributions.

From her earliest days, Minakshi was distinguished by an insatiable appetite for reading. Her literary universe was inhabited by characters and narratives that spanned ethical tales, motivational and inspirational stories, and the mythic parables imbued with life lessons. This voracious reading habit was not merely for personal edification but was driven by a desire to distill and disseminate the essence of these narratives to foster the development of students and peers alike. She was particularly captivated by the lives and teachings of historical figures and spiritual leaders such as Adi Shankaracharya, Swami Vivekananda, Dr. APJ Abdul Kalam, Mahamana Pandit Madan Mohan Malviya, Mahatma Gandhi, Sardar Vallabhai Patel, and Vinoba Bhave, among others. Their philosophies and life stories fueled her ambition to embody their ideals of resilience, selflessness, and relentless pursuit of knowledge.

Dr. Minakshi's academic and practical engagement with psychology has been equally noteworthy. As a research scholar, her focus has been on exploring the intricate tapestry of the human psyche, aiming to unlock the potential for psychological well-being and societal harmony. Her scholarly work is complemented by her active involvement in social work, where she employs her academic insights to make tangible differences in the lives of the underprivileged. Her endeavours in social work are characterized by an innovative approach that combines traditional wisdom with contemporary psychological practices to address the multifaceted challenges faced by these communities.

Her artistic talents, another facet of her diverse capabilities, are not merely a personal passion but also serve as a medium through which she communicates and connects with others. Her art, rich in symbolism and emotional depth, reflects her philosophical inquiries and social concerns, offering viewers a glimpse into the breadth of her intellect and the depth of her compassion.

In addition to her contributions to the arts and social sciences, Dr. Minakshi has embraced the healing arts of Pranic Healing, mastering the techniques developed by Master Choa Kok Sui. This practice, which focuses on the manipulation of Prana or life energy to heal the body and aura, has been both a personal journey of discovery and a means through which she extends her healing touch to others. Her proficiency in Pranic Healing is complemented by her advocacy and teaching of various forms of meditation aimed at rejuvenation, personal betterment, and the cultivation of harmony within individuals and communities alike.

Dr. Minakshi's life is a narrative of relentless pursuit, not just of personal achievement but of the upliftment and empowerment of society at large. Her diverse interests and talents—spanning the arts, literature, psychology, and the healing practices—converge on a singular path of service. She embodies the spirit of the luminaries who inspired her, channelling their legacy through her actions and teachings. Through her books, art, and social initiatives, she continues to inspire a new generation to embark on their own journeys of self-discovery, resilience, and altruism.

Her commitment to social betterment, particularly her focus on uplifting underprivileged children, reflects a deep understanding of the transformative potential of education and personal development. By integrating her knowledge of psychology, her artistic sensibilities, and her healing practices, Dr. Bansal has developed a holistic approach to social work that addresses both the immediate needs and the long-term well-being of the communities she serves.

As an author, Dr. Minakshi's writings offer a blend of inspirational insights, practical wisdom, and reflective contemplations drawn from her extensive reading and life experiences. Her books serve as a guide for those seeking to navigate the complexities of life with grace, resilience, and purpose. Through her narratives, she extends an invitation to her readers to explore the depths of their own potential and to contribute meaningfully to the collective well-being of society.

In Dr. Minakshi Bansal, we find a remarkable synthesis of the artist, the scholar, the healer, and the social activist. Her life's work stands as a beacon of hope and a source of inspiration for individuals seeking to make a difference in the world. Her story is a compelling reminder of the power of individual action, rooted in compassion and driven by a profound commitment to the betterment of humanity. Dr. Minakshi's legacy is not just in the tangible outcomes of her efforts but in the enduring spirit of inquiry, empathy, and service that she embodies.

ᐳᐳᐳ

# Preface

As I embark on the journey of writing this book, I find myself reflecting on the profound transformations that have shaped the business world over recent years. The rapid pace of technological advancements, coupled with shifts in societal values and consumer behaviors, has created a landscape that is both exhilarating and daunting. This book, "The Future is Now: Emerging Trends in Business," is a culmination of my observations, research, and insights into the forces that are redefining how businesses operate, compete, and grow. It is a testament to the dynamic nature of our times, where change is the only constant and innovation the key to survival and success.

The impetus for this book emerged from my deep-seated curiosity and passion for understanding the intricacies of the modern business environment. As someone who has spent years studying and analyzing business trends, I have witnessed firsthand the transformative power of technology, the evolving expectations of consumers, and the imperative for businesses to adopt sustainable and ethical practices. These experiences have shaped my belief that the future of business lies at the intersection of innovation, responsibility, and adaptability.

In writing this book, I aimed to provide a comprehensive exploration of the emerging trends that are shaping the future of business. Each chapter delves into a specific trend, offering a detailed analysis of its implications, challenges, and opportunities. From the digital transformation and the rise of artificial intelligence to the ethics of innovation and corporate social responsibility, this book seeks to paint a holistic picture of the forces driving change in the business world. My goal is to equip readers with the knowledge and insights they need to navigate this complex landscape and harness these trends to their advantage.

One of the central themes that runs throughout this book is the transformative potential of technology. We are living in an era where digital technologies are fundamentally altering how businesses operate and interact with their stakeholders. The advent of big data, cloud computing, and the Internet of Things has revolutionized processes, enabling businesses to operate more efficiently and make more informed decisions. Artificial intelligence and machine learning are taking this transformation a step further, providing unprecedented capabilities for analyzing data, predicting trends, and automating tasks. These technologies are not just enhancing operational efficiency; they are also creating new business models and opportunities for innovation.

However, the integration of technology into business operations also brings its own set of challenges and ethical considerations. Cybersecurity has become a critical concern as businesses grapple with the need to protect their digital assets from increasingly sophisticated cyber threats. Ensuring data privacy and security is paramount, especially as consumers become more aware of their rights and more concerned about how their personal information is used. Moreover, the deployment of artificial intelligence raises questions about bias, transparency, and accountability. As businesses harness the power of AI, they must also take steps to ensure that these technologies are used responsibly and ethically.

Another key theme explored in this book is the shifting expectations of consumers and the imperative for businesses to adapt accordingly. Today's consumers are more informed, empowered, and discerning than ever before. They expect brands to not only provide high-quality products and services but also to align with their values and contribute positively to society. This has given rise to the importance of corporate social responsibility, as businesses strive to demonstrate their commitment to ethical practices, environmental sustainability, and social impact. Companies that prioritize these aspects are more likely to build trust, foster loyalty, and gain a competitive edge.

Sustainability is no longer a niche concern but a mainstream expectation. Businesses across industries are recognizing the need to adopt sustainable practices to address environmental challenges and meet the demands of conscious consumers. This involves rethinking supply chains, reducing waste, and investing in renewable energy. Sustainable business practices are not only beneficial for the planet but also for the bottom line, as they can lead to cost savings, innovation, and improved brand reputation. By embracing sustainability, businesses can contribute to a more sustainable future while enhancing their long-term viability.

The evolution of the workforce is another significant trend discussed in this book. The rise of the gig economy and remote work has redefined traditional employment models, offering flexibility and autonomy to workers. However, these changes also raise important questions about job security, benefits, and workers' rights. Balancing the benefits of flexible work arrangements with the need for fair labor practices is crucial for creating a sustainable and equitable workforce. Additionally, the integration of technology into the workplace is reshaping the skills required for success, highlighting the importance of continuous learning and professional development.

The role of corporate social responsibility in shaping business strategies is a recurrent theme throughout this book. Businesses are increasingly recognizing that their responsibilities extend beyond profit maximization to include social, environmental, and ethical considerations. This shift is driven by a growing awareness of the interconnectedness of business and society, as well as the recognition that sustainable practices can lead to long-term success. Companies that embrace corporate social responsibility are better positioned to build strong relationships with stakeholders, enhance their reputation, and contribute to the well-being of society.

The ethics of innovation is a topic that warrants careful consideration, as the rapid pace of technological advancement often outstrips the development of ethical guidelines and regulatory frameworks. Innovators must navigate complex ethical dilemmas, balancing the potential benefits of new technologies with the need to minimize harm and ensure fairness. This involves conducting thorough risk assessments, engaging with diverse stakeholders, and adhering to ethical principles. By prioritizing ethical innovation, businesses can build trust and ensure that their advancements contribute positively to society.

The blending of online and offline worlds is a trend that is reshaping the retail landscape. Omnichannel retailing, which integrates digital and physical retail spaces, offers consumers a seamless and convenient shopping experience. Technologies such as augmented reality and artificial intelligence are enhancing the retail experience, providing personalized recommendations, virtual try-ons, and efficient supply chain management. By leveraging these technologies, retailers can create engaging and immersive experiences that meet the diverse needs of modern consumers. The future of retail lies in the ability to seamlessly integrate online and offline channels, creating a cohesive and responsive shopping experience.

Education and learning are undergoing significant transformations, driven by advancements in educational technology. Digital platforms and tools are making education more accessible, flexible, and personalized. Students can learn at their own pace, access a wealth of resources, and engage with interactive content. The integration of technology into education supports lifelong learning and prepares individuals for the demands of the digital age. However, addressing challenges such as digital equity, student engagement, and data privacy is essential for maximizing the benefits of educational technology.

Healthcare is another sector experiencing profound changes due to technological advancements. Health tech innovations such as telemedicine, wearable devices, artificial intelligence, and blockchain are improving access, efficiency, and patient outcomes. These technologies enable remote consultations, continuous health monitoring, personalized treatment plans, and secure data management. By integrating health tech innovations into healthcare systems, providers can enhance the quality of care, reduce costs, and improve patient experiences. Ensuring ethical considerations, such as data privacy and equitable access, is crucial for the responsible deployment of health tech.

The sharing economy is promoting collaborative consumption by enabling individuals to share access to goods and services. Platforms like Airbnb, Uber, and Rent the Runway facilitate peer-to-peer exchanges, providing flexibility and cost savings for users. The sharing economy leverages underutilized assets, reduces waste, and fosters community engagement. However, it also raises challenges related to regulation, labor rights, and data privacy. Balancing the benefits of the sharing economy with the need for fair and ethical practices is essential for creating a sustainable and equitable model of collaborative consumption.

As I reflect on the themes explored in this book, I am struck by the interconnectedness of these trends and their collective impact on the future of business. The convergence of technology, ethics, sustainability, and social responsibility is creating a new paradigm for business success. Companies that navigate these trends effectively, prioritizing innovation, responsibility, and adaptability, are well-positioned to thrive in the dynamic and ever-evolving business landscape.

Writing this book has been a deeply enriching experience, allowing me to delve into the complexities of the modern business world and explore the forces shaping its future. It is my hope that this book provides valuable insights and guidance to business leaders, entrepreneurs, and anyone interested in understanding the emerging trends in business. The future is now, and the decisions we make today will shape the world of tomorrow. By embracing these trends with a sense of responsibility and a commitment to ethical practices, we can create a future that is not only prosperous but also just, sustainable, and inclusive.

As we move forward, it is important to remember that the journey of innovation is continuous, and the landscape will keep evolving. Staying informed, adaptable, and ethically grounded will be key to navigating this journey successfully. I invite readers to join me in exploring the fascinating world of emerging business trends and to consider how we can collectively contribute to shaping a better future.

*Dr. Minakshi Bansal*
*Social Activist*
*Ahmedabad, Gujarat, Bharat*

# ONE

# THE DIGITAL TRANSFORMATION - EMBRACING TECHNOLOGY FOR COMPETITIVE ADVANTAGE

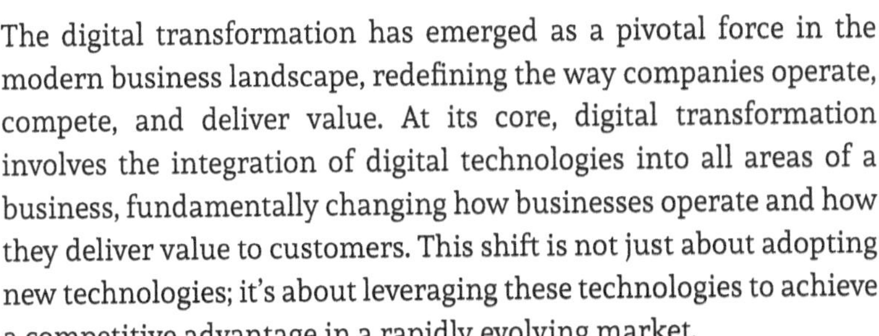

The digital transformation has emerged as a pivotal force in the modern business landscape, redefining the way companies operate, compete, and deliver value. At its core, digital transformation involves the integration of digital technologies into all areas of a business, fundamentally changing how businesses operate and how they deliver value to customers. This shift is not just about adopting new technologies; it's about leveraging these technologies to achieve a competitive advantage in a rapidly evolving market.

Embracing digital transformation begins with understanding its scope and impact. Digital transformation encompasses a wide range of technologies, including artificial intelligence (AI), machine learning, big data, cloud computing, the Internet of Things (IoT), and blockchain, among others. These technologies enable businesses to streamline operations, enhance customer experiences, and create new revenue streams. By adopting these technologies, businesses can improve efficiency, reduce costs, and gain insights that were previously unattainable.

One of the primary drivers of digital transformation is the need to stay competitive in an increasingly digital world. Traditional business models are being disrupted by agile, technology-driven startups that leverage digital tools to offer better products and services at lower costs. Established companies must adapt or risk being left behind. Digital transformation allows businesses to remain relevant by adopting innovative strategies and processes that improve their ability to compete.

A key aspect of digital transformation is the use of data to drive decision-making. The explosion of data in recent years has created opportunities for businesses to gain deeper insights into their operations and customer behaviors. By leveraging big data analytics, companies can make more informed decisions, optimize their processes, and tailor their offerings to meet the specific needs of their customers. For instance, data analytics can help businesses identify trends and patterns that can inform product development, marketing strategies, and customer service improvements.

Another critical component of digital transformation is the enhancement of customer experiences. In today's digital age, customers expect seamless, personalized interactions with brands across all touchpoints. Businesses that can deliver on these expectations are more likely to build strong, loyal customer relationships. Digital technologies enable companies to create personalized experiences by analyzing customer data and using it to tailor interactions and offers. For example, AI-driven chatbots can provide personalized customer support, while recommendation engines can suggest products based on past purchases and browsing behavior.

Digital transformation also plays a crucial role in operational efficiency. By automating routine tasks and processes, businesses can reduce costs and improve productivity. Automation technologies, such as robotic process automation (RPA), can handle repetitive tasks, freeing up employees to focus on more strategic activities. Additionally, cloud computing allows businesses to scale their operations quickly and efficiently, providing the flexibility needed to respond to changing market conditions.

Moreover, digital transformation fosters innovation by enabling businesses to experiment with new ideas and business models. The agility provided by digital technologies allows companies to quickly test and iterate on new concepts, reducing the time and cost associated with bringing new products and services to market. This innovation is essential for staying ahead of the competition and meeting the ever-evolving needs of customers.

Security is another critical aspect of digital transformation. As businesses become more reliant on digital technologies, the need to protect sensitive data and systems becomes paramount. Cybersecurity measures must be integrated into every aspect of the digital transformation strategy to safeguard against threats and ensure the integrity of business operations. This includes implementing robust security protocols, conducting regular risk assessments, and educating employees about cybersecurity best practices.

The successful implementation of digital transformation requires a cultural shift within the organization. It involves more than just technology adoption; it requires a change in mindset and the willingness to embrace new ways of working. Leadership plays a crucial role in driving this change by fostering a culture of innovation, encouraging experimentation, and promoting continuous learning. Employees at all levels must be engaged and empowered to contribute to the digital transformation efforts.

One of the most significant challenges businesses face in digital transformation is the integration of new technologies with existing systems. Legacy systems can be difficult to replace and may not be compatible with modern digital solutions. Businesses must develop strategies to integrate new technologies seamlessly, whether through gradual migration, the use of middleware, or adopting a hybrid approach that combines old and new systems. This integration is essential for ensuring a smooth transition and maximizing the benefits of digital transformation.

Digital transformation also requires a significant investment in technology and talent. Businesses must allocate resources to acquire the necessary digital tools and technologies, as well as to train employees to use them effectively. Investing in employee training and development is crucial for building the digital skills needed to support transformation efforts. Additionally, businesses may need to hire new talent with specialized skills in areas such as data analytics, cybersecurity, and AI to drive their digital initiatives.

One of the most compelling examples of digital transformation is the retail industry. Traditional brick-and-mortar retailers have had to adapt to the rise of e-commerce and changing consumer behaviors. By embracing digital technologies, retailers can enhance the shopping experience, streamline operations, and create new revenue streams. For instance, retailers use data analytics to understand customer preferences and tailor their marketing efforts, while AI-powered chatbots provide personalized customer support. Additionally, technologies like augmented reality (AR) and virtual reality (VR) are being used to create immersive shopping experiences that bridge the gap between online and in-store shopping.

The healthcare industry is another sector that has benefited significantly from digital transformation. Digital technologies are revolutionizing healthcare delivery by improving patient care, enhancing operational efficiency, and enabling new treatments and therapies. For example, telemedicine allows patients to consult with healthcare providers remotely, improving access to care and reducing the need for in-person visits. AI and machine learning are being used to analyze medical data and assist in diagnosis and treatment planning. Furthermore, IoT devices, such as wearable health monitors, enable continuous monitoring of patients' health, providing real-time data that can be used to manage chronic conditions and improve outcomes.

The financial services industry has also undergone significant digital transformation. Fintech innovations are disrupting traditional banking models by offering faster, more convenient, and cost-effective financial services. Digital payment systems, peer-to-peer lending platforms, and blockchain-based solutions are just a few examples of how technology is reshaping the financial landscape. These innovations enable financial institutions to enhance customer experiences, improve operational efficiency, and create new business opportunities.

Manufacturing is another industry that is being transformed by digital technologies. The concept of Industry 4.0 refers to the integration of digital technologies, such as IoT, AI, and robotics, into manufacturing processes. This transformation enables manufacturers to optimize production, improve quality, and reduce costs. For instance, IoT sensors can monitor equipment performance in real-time, allowing for predictive maintenance that minimizes downtime. AI algorithms can analyze production data to identify inefficiencies and suggest improvements. Additionally, advanced robotics and automation technologies can increase precision and speed in manufacturing processes.

The transportation and logistics industry is also experiencing a digital revolution. Technologies such as IoT, AI, and big data analytics are being used to optimize supply chain operations, improve fleet management, and enhance customer experiences. For example, IoT sensors can track the location and condition of goods in transit, providing real-time visibility into the supply chain. AI algorithms can analyze traffic patterns and optimize delivery routes, reducing transportation costs and improving delivery times. Additionally, digital platforms are enabling new business models, such as ride-sharing and on-demand delivery services, that are reshaping the transportation landscape.

Education is another sector that is being transformed by digital technologies. The rise of EdTech has enabled new approaches to teaching and learning that enhance educational experiences and outcomes. Online learning platforms, digital classrooms, and AI-driven tutoring systems are just a few examples of how technology is reshaping education. These innovations provide greater access to education, personalized learning experiences, and new opportunities for collaboration and engagement. Furthermore, digital credentials and blockchain-based certification systems are being used to validate and verify educational achievements, providing greater transparency and trust in the education system.

The hospitality industry is also benefiting from digital transformation. Digital technologies are enhancing guest experiences, streamlining operations, and enabling new business models. For instance, hotels use AI-powered chatbots to provide personalized customer service, while IoT devices enable smart room features, such as automated lighting and temperature control. Additionally, digital platforms are enabling new business models, such as vacation rentals and peer-to-peer lodging, that are disrupting traditional hospitality models. These innovations enable hotels and other hospitality providers to offer more personalized, convenient, and cost-effective services to their guests.

In the media and entertainment industry, digital transformation is enabling new ways of creating, distributing, and consuming content. Streaming platforms, social media, and digital content creation tools are just a few examples of how technology is reshaping the industry. These innovations provide greater access to content, new opportunities for engagement, and new revenue streams for content creators. Additionally, technologies such as AI and VR are being used to create immersive and interactive experiences that enhance audience engagement.

Overall, digital transformation is a critical driver of competitive advantage in today's business environment. By embracing digital technologies, businesses can improve efficiency, enhance customer experiences, and create new opportunities for growth. However, successful digital transformation requires more than just technology adoption; it requires a cultural shift, strategic integration, and significant investment in technology and talent. Businesses that can navigate these challenges and leverage digital technologies effectively will be well-positioned to thrive in the digital age.

ϸϸϸ

*"Innovation is the lifeblood of progress, but it must be guided by ethics and responsibility. The future of business depends on balancing technological advancements with social good. Let us innovate with integrity and purpose."*

# TWO

# AI and Machine Learning - Revolutionizing Business Intelligence

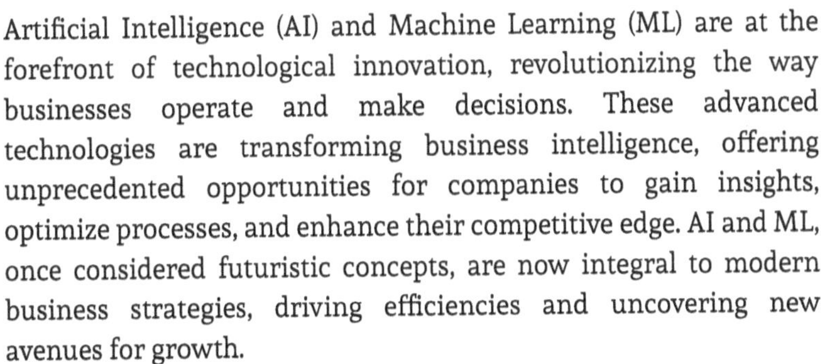

Artificial Intelligence (AI) and Machine Learning (ML) are at the forefront of technological innovation, revolutionizing the way businesses operate and make decisions. These advanced technologies are transforming business intelligence, offering unprecedented opportunities for companies to gain insights, optimize processes, and enhance their competitive edge. AI and ML, once considered futuristic concepts, are now integral to modern business strategies, driving efficiencies and uncovering new avenues for growth.

At the heart of AI and ML is the ability to process vast amounts of data quickly and accurately. Traditional data analysis methods often fall short when dealing with the sheer volume and complexity of today's data. AI and ML, however, excel in this area. AI refers to the simulation of human intelligence in machines that are programmed to think and learn. ML, a subset of AI, involves the use of algorithms and statistical models to enable computers to improve their performance on a task through experience. Together, these technologies enable businesses to analyze large datasets, identify patterns, and make data-driven decisions with remarkable speed and precision.

One of the most significant impacts of AI and ML on business intelligence is the enhancement of predictive analytics. Predictive analytics involves using historical data to make predictions about future events. AI and ML algorithms can analyze past performance, identify trends, and forecast future outcomes with a high degree of accuracy. This capability is invaluable for businesses, allowing them to anticipate market trends, customer behaviors, and operational challenges. For example, in the retail industry, predictive analytics can help companies forecast demand for products, optimize inventory levels, and improve supply chain efficiency. In finance, it can be used to predict stock prices, assess credit risk, and detect fraudulent activities.

Another critical application of AI and ML in business intelligence is in the realm of customer insights. Understanding customer preferences, behaviors, and needs is essential for businesses to create personalized experiences and build customer loyalty. AI and ML can analyze customer data from various sources, such as social media, purchase history, and website interactions, to create detailed customer profiles. These profiles enable businesses to segment their audience, tailor marketing campaigns, and deliver personalized recommendations. For instance, streaming services like Netflix and music platforms like Spotify use AI and ML to analyze user data and provide personalized content recommendations, enhancing user engagement and satisfaction.

Operational efficiency is another area where AI and ML are making a significant impact. By automating routine tasks and optimizing processes, these technologies can reduce costs and improve productivity. In manufacturing, AI-powered robots and ML algorithms are used to monitor equipment performance, predict maintenance needs, and optimize production schedules. This predictive maintenance can prevent equipment failures, reduce downtime, and extend the lifespan of machinery. In logistics, AI and ML can optimize routing, manage inventory, and forecast demand, ensuring that goods are delivered on time and at the lowest possible cost.

AI and ML are also transforming the financial services industry. In banking, these technologies are used to automate customer service, detect fraud, and assess creditworthiness. Chatbots powered by AI can handle routine customer inquiries, freeing up human agents to focus on more complex issues. ML algorithms can analyze transaction data to detect unusual patterns that may indicate fraudulent activity. Additionally, AI and ML can assess credit risk by analyzing a wide range of data points, including social media activity and online behavior, providing a more comprehensive view of a customer's creditworthiness than traditional methods.

In healthcare, AI and ML are revolutionizing diagnostics, treatment planning, and patient care. These technologies can analyze medical images, such as X-rays and MRIs, to detect anomalies and assist in diagnosis. They can also analyze patient data to predict disease progression, identify potential complications, and recommend personalized treatment plans. For example, AI-powered diagnostic tools can detect early signs of diseases like cancer, enabling timely intervention and improving patient outcomes. In addition, ML algorithms can analyze data from wearable devices to monitor patients' health in real-time, alerting healthcare providers to any significant changes that may require attention.

The integration of AI and ML into business intelligence also brings about enhanced decision-making capabilities. By providing actionable insights derived from data, these technologies enable businesses to make informed decisions quickly. For instance, AI-driven analytics platforms can provide real-time dashboards that highlight key performance indicators and alert decision-makers to any significant changes. This real-time visibility allows businesses to respond swiftly to emerging trends, capitalize on opportunities, and mitigate risks. Furthermore, AI and ML can perform scenario analysis, simulating various business scenarios and predicting their outcomes, helping businesses plan for different contingencies and make strategic decisions with greater confidence.

Marketing is another domain where AI and ML are driving significant transformations. These technologies enable marketers to analyze consumer data and behavior, optimize campaigns, and measure their effectiveness. AI-powered tools can automate tasks such as audience segmentation, content creation, and ad placement, ensuring that marketing efforts are both targeted and efficient. For example, AI algorithms can analyze social media activity to identify trends and sentiments, allowing marketers to tailor their messaging accordingly. Additionally, ML models can predict the success of marketing campaigns by analyzing historical data, helping marketers allocate their budgets more effectively and achieve better returns on investment.

The power of AI and ML extends to enhancing cybersecurity measures. As cyber threats become more sophisticated, traditional security measures are often inadequate. AI and ML can analyze vast amounts of data to identify patterns and detect anomalies that may indicate a security breach. These technologies can also learn from past incidents to predict and prevent future attacks. For example, ML algorithms can analyze network traffic to detect unusual activity that may signal a cyber attack. By identifying threats in real-time, businesses can respond more quickly and effectively, minimizing the potential impact of security breaches.

Supply chain management is another area benefiting from AI and ML. These technologies can optimize various aspects of the supply chain, from procurement to distribution. AI-powered analytics can forecast demand, optimize inventory levels, and improve supplier selection. ML algorithms can analyze data from various sources, such as weather reports, market trends, and geopolitical events, to predict potential disruptions and suggest contingency plans. This proactive approach ensures that supply chains are more resilient and can adapt to changing conditions, reducing the risk of delays and ensuring timely delivery of goods.

Despite the numerous benefits, the implementation of AI and ML in business intelligence is not without challenges. One of the primary challenges is data quality. AI and ML algorithms rely on large volumes of high-quality data to function effectively. Inaccurate, incomplete, or biased data can lead to erroneous insights and flawed decision-making. Therefore, businesses must invest in robust data management practices to ensure that their data is accurate, comprehensive, and free from bias. This includes data cleaning, integration, and validation processes, as well as the use of advanced data governance frameworks.

Another challenge is the integration of AI and ML into existing business processes and systems. Many businesses operate with legacy systems that may not be compatible with modern AI and ML solutions. This integration requires significant investment in technology infrastructure and may involve redesigning business processes to accommodate new technologies. Additionally, businesses must ensure that their employees have the necessary skills to work with AI and ML tools. This may involve training existing staff, hiring new talent, or partnering with external experts to bridge the skills gap.

Ethical considerations also play a crucial role in the adoption of AI and ML. These technologies can raise concerns related to privacy, transparency, and accountability. For example, AI algorithms that make decisions based on personal data must be designed to protect individuals' privacy and comply with data protection regulations. Additionally, the decision-making processes of AI systems must be transparent and explainable, ensuring that businesses can justify their actions and be held accountable for any adverse outcomes. Addressing these ethical considerations is essential for building trust with customers, employees, and other stakeholders.

The rapid advancement of AI and ML technologies also means that businesses must continuously adapt to stay ahead. These technologies are evolving at a fast pace, and businesses that fail to keep up with the latest developments risk falling behind their competitors. Continuous learning and innovation are therefore essential for maintaining a competitive edge. Businesses must stay informed about the latest trends in AI and ML, experiment with new applications, and be willing to invest in research and development to drive innovation.

The future of AI and ML in business intelligence holds even more promise. As these technologies continue to advance, their capabilities will expand, offering new opportunities for businesses to enhance their operations and gain a competitive advantage. For example, advancements in natural language processing (NLP) will enable AI systems to understand and interpret human language more accurately, improving customer interactions and enabling more sophisticated data analysis. Similarly, developments in reinforcement learning, a type of ML that involves training algorithms through trial and error, will enable AI systems to learn more effectively and adapt to complex environments.

In conclusion, AI and ML are revolutionizing business intelligence by providing powerful tools for data analysis, predictive analytics, customer insights, operational efficiency, and decision-making. These technologies offer significant benefits, including enhanced accuracy, speed, and scalability, enabling businesses to gain a competitive edge in a rapidly evolving market. However, the successful implementation of AI and ML requires careful consideration of data quality, integration challenges, ethical considerations, and the need for continuous innovation. Businesses that can navigate these challenges and leverage the full potential of AI and ML will be well-positioned to thrive in the digital age, driving growth, efficiency, and customer satisfaction.

"The digital transformation of business is not just about technology; it's about reimagining possibilities. Embrace change, but always consider the human element. Technology should enhance our lives, not complicate them."

# THREE

## BLOCKCHAIN BEYOND BITCOIN - SECURING TRANSACTIONS AND TRUST

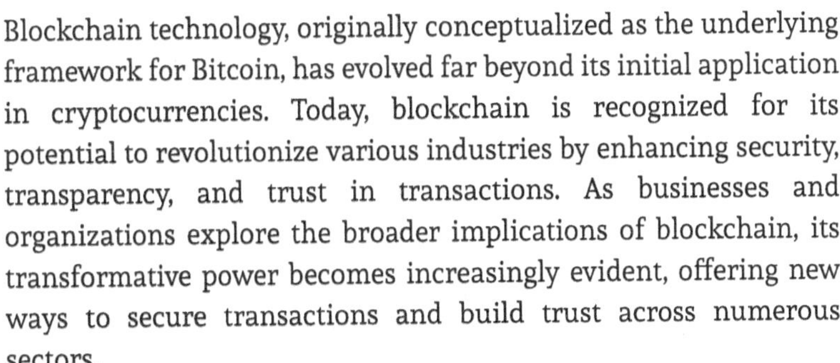

Blockchain technology, originally conceptualized as the underlying framework for Bitcoin, has evolved far beyond its initial application in cryptocurrencies. Today, blockchain is recognized for its potential to revolutionize various industries by enhancing security, transparency, and trust in transactions. As businesses and organizations explore the broader implications of blockchain, its transformative power becomes increasingly evident, offering new ways to secure transactions and build trust across numerous sectors.

At its core, blockchain is a decentralized digital ledger that records transactions across a network of computers in a way that ensures the data's integrity and security. Each transaction is grouped with others into a "block," which is then added to a chronological "chain" of previous blocks. This structure makes it nearly impossible to alter any information without altering all subsequent blocks, thus ensuring the data's immutability. The decentralized nature of blockchain means that no single entity controls the entire network, reducing the risk of fraud and enhancing trust among participants.

One of the primary advantages of blockchain technology is its ability to secure transactions. Traditional transaction systems often rely on centralized intermediaries, such as banks or payment processors, to validate and record transactions. This centralization can create vulnerabilities, as a single point of failure can be targeted by hackers or suffer from operational issues. Blockchain eliminates the need for these intermediaries by using cryptographic algorithms to validate transactions. Each transaction is verified by multiple participants in the network, known as nodes, through a consensus mechanism. This distributed verification process ensures that transactions are secure, transparent, and resistant to tampering.

Beyond financial transactions, blockchain technology is being applied to enhance security and trust in various other contexts. One significant application is in supply chain management. Traditional supply chains are often complex, involving multiple parties across different regions, which can lead to inefficiencies, fraud, and a lack of transparency. Blockchain can streamline supply chains by providing a single, immutable record of all transactions and movements of goods. For example, a product's journey from manufacturer to consumer can be tracked on a blockchain, with each step recorded in a tamper-proof ledger. This transparency helps prevent fraud, such as counterfeit goods, and improves efficiency by reducing the need for manual record-keeping and verification.

In the realm of digital identity, blockchain offers a secure and decentralized solution for managing personal information. Traditional identity systems often rely on centralized databases that can be vulnerable to breaches and unauthorized access. Blockchain-based identity systems, on the other hand, store identity information in a decentralized manner, giving individuals control over their data. Users can share only the necessary information with third parties, such as financial institutions or healthcare providers, without revealing their entire identity. This approach enhances privacy and security, reducing the risk of identity theft and fraud.

Blockchain's potential to revolutionize the healthcare industry is another area of growing interest. Healthcare systems often struggle with issues related to data interoperability, security, and patient privacy. Blockchain can address these challenges by providing a secure, decentralized platform for storing and sharing medical records. Patients can have control over their health data, granting access to healthcare providers as needed while ensuring that their information remains private and secure. Moreover, blockchain can facilitate the secure sharing of data between different healthcare organizations, improving collaboration and enhancing the quality of care.

The financial industry, where blockchain technology first gained prominence, continues to explore and implement blockchain solutions beyond cryptocurrencies. One notable application is in cross-border payments. Traditional international payment systems can be slow, costly, and opaque, often requiring several days for transactions to clear and involving multiple intermediaries. Blockchain technology can streamline this process by enabling near-instantaneous, low-cost cross-border transactions. For example, Ripple, a blockchain-based payment protocol, allows for real-time, secure international payments, reducing the need for correspondent banks and lowering transaction fees.

Smart contracts represent another groundbreaking application of blockchain technology. Smart contracts are self-executing contracts with the terms of the agreement directly written into code. These contracts automatically execute and enforce themselves when predetermined conditions are met. By eliminating the need for intermediaries, smart contracts can reduce costs, increase efficiency, and minimize the potential for disputes. For instance, in real estate transactions, a smart contract could automate the transfer of property ownership once the payment is received, ensuring that all parties comply with the agreement terms.

Blockchain's transparency and security features make it a valuable tool for enhancing trust in various sectors. In the voting process, for example, blockchain can provide a secure and transparent platform for casting and counting votes, reducing the risk of fraud and ensuring the integrity of the election. Each vote can be recorded on a blockchain, creating an immutable and auditable trail that can be verified by all participants. This approach can enhance voter confidence and improve the overall transparency of the electoral process.

The art and entertainment industries are also exploring blockchain to address issues related to ownership and copyright. Artists and creators often face challenges in proving ownership and receiving fair compensation for their work. Blockchain can provide a transparent and immutable record of ownership, enabling creators to establish and protect their rights. For example, non-fungible tokens (NFTs) are digital assets that represent ownership of unique items, such as digital art, music, or collectibles. NFTs are stored on a blockchain, ensuring that the ownership and provenance of the digital asset are transparent and verifiable.

In the realm of charitable donations and nonprofit organizations, blockchain can enhance transparency and accountability. Donors often seek assurance that their contributions are being used effectively and for the intended purposes. Blockchain can provide a transparent ledger of donations and expenditures, allowing donors to track how their funds are being utilized. This transparency can build trust and encourage more donations, ultimately benefiting the organizations and the causes they support.

Despite the numerous benefits and applications of blockchain technology, its adoption is not without challenges. One of the primary obstacles is scalability. As the number of transactions on a blockchain network increases, the time and computational power required to process and validate these transactions can become significant. This can lead to slower transaction times and higher costs, particularly on public blockchains with large networks. To address this challenge, various solutions, such as sharding and layer-2 protocols, are being developed to improve blockchain scalability and efficiency.

Another challenge is the regulatory environment surrounding blockchain technology. As blockchain applications expand into various industries, they must comply with existing regulations and adapt to new ones. Regulatory uncertainty can hinder the adoption and development of blockchain solutions, as businesses may be hesitant to invest in technology that could face legal obstacles. To overcome this challenge, it is essential for regulators and industry stakeholders to collaborate and establish clear, supportive regulatory frameworks that promote innovation while ensuring consumer protection and compliance.

The energy consumption associated with blockchain networks, particularly those using proof-of-work (PoW) consensus mechanisms, is another concern. PoW, used by Bitcoin and other cryptocurrencies, requires significant computational power to solve complex mathematical problems and validate transactions. This process consumes substantial amounts of electricity, raising environmental concerns. To address this issue, alternative consensus mechanisms, such as proof-of-stake (PoS), are being explored. PoS requires less energy by allowing validators to create new blocks based on the number of tokens they hold and are willing to "stake" as collateral. These alternatives aim to reduce the environmental impact of blockchain technology while maintaining security and decentralization.

Interoperability between different blockchain networks is also a critical challenge. As various blockchains are developed for different purposes and industries, the ability for these networks to communicate and interact with one another becomes essential. Interoperability solutions, such as cross-chain protocols and interoperability standards, are being developed to enable seamless communication between different blockchain networks. This will allow for the exchange of assets and information across multiple blockchains, enhancing the overall utility and adoption of blockchain technology.

Education and awareness are crucial for the widespread adoption of blockchain technology. Many businesses and individuals are still unfamiliar with how blockchain works and its potential benefits. To address this knowledge gap, educational initiatives and resources are needed to provide a clear understanding of blockchain technology, its applications, and its impact on various industries. By increasing awareness and understanding, businesses and individuals can make informed decisions about adopting and implementing blockchain solutions.

Looking ahead, the future of blockchain technology is promising, with ongoing advancements and innovations poised to address current challenges and unlock new possibilities. As blockchain continues to mature, its potential to revolutionize industries and enhance security and trust in transactions will become increasingly apparent. Businesses that embrace blockchain technology and leverage its capabilities will be well-positioned to navigate the evolving digital landscape, gain a competitive edge, and build lasting trust with their stakeholders.

The potential of blockchain extends beyond its initial association with Bitcoin and cryptocurrencies. Its applications in securing transactions and building trust across various sectors demonstrate its transformative power. By providing a decentralized, transparent, and secure platform, blockchain technology offers significant advantages in enhancing efficiency, reducing fraud, and fostering trust. While challenges remain, ongoing innovations and collaborations are paving the way for broader adoption and integration of blockchain technology into everyday business practices. As businesses and organizations continue to explore and implement blockchain solutions, the technology's full potential will be realized, driving a new era of secure and trusted transactions.

# FOUR

# THE GIG ECONOMY – REDEFINING THE WORKFORCE LANDSCAPE

The gig economy has emerged as a transformative force in the modern workforce, redefining traditional employment models and reshaping how people work and businesses operate. Characterized by short-term contracts, freelance work, and independent contracting, the gig economy offers flexibility and autonomy for workers while providing businesses with a dynamic and adaptable labor force. This shift has profound implications for the workforce landscape, impacting job security, benefits, and the nature of work itself.

At its core, the gig economy is driven by digital platforms that connect workers with short-term jobs or projects. Companies like Uber, Lyft, Airbnb, and TaskRabbit have pioneered this model, enabling individuals to offer their services directly to consumers through user-friendly apps and websites. These platforms facilitate a wide range of gigs, from ride-sharing and food delivery to home repairs and freelance writing. By leveraging technology, they streamline the process of finding and completing gigs, making it easier for workers to access opportunities and for businesses to meet their needs quickly and efficiently.

One of the most significant advantages of the gig economy is the flexibility it offers workers. Unlike traditional employment, gig work allows individuals to set their own schedules and choose the projects they take on. This flexibility is particularly appealing to those who seek a better work-life balance or need to accommodate other responsibilities, such as caregiving or education. For example, a ride-share driver can decide when to log into the app and accept rides, while a freelance graphic designer can choose which clients to work with and when to complete assignments. This level of control over one's work schedule is a major draw for many gig workers, enabling them to tailor their work to their personal needs and preferences.

The gig economy also provides opportunities for individuals to diversify their income streams. Rather than relying on a single employer, gig workers can take on multiple gigs simultaneously, spreading their income sources across different platforms and clients. This diversification can offer a form of financial security, as workers are not solely dependent on one job for their livelihood. Additionally, it allows individuals to pursue their passions and interests, often turning hobbies or skills into profitable ventures. For instance, a person with a talent for photography can take freelance photography gigs, while also working as a part-time delivery driver.

For businesses, the gig economy offers a flexible and cost-effective way to access talent. Companies can hire gig workers on a project-by-project basis, scaling their workforce up or down as needed without the long-term commitments associated with full-time employees. This adaptability is particularly valuable in industries with fluctuating demand, where businesses may need to respond quickly to changing market conditions. By tapping into the gig economy, companies can access a diverse pool of talent with specialized skills, filling gaps in their workforce and addressing specific needs without the overhead costs of traditional employment.

However, the rise of the gig economy also presents significant challenges and raises important questions about the future of work. One of the most pressing issues is job security. Unlike traditional employees, gig workers do not have guaranteed hours or stable income, making it difficult to predict their financial situation from one month to the next. This lack of stability can be particularly challenging for individuals who rely on gig work as their primary source of income. Without the safety net of a regular paycheck, gig workers may face financial uncertainty, especially during periods of low demand or economic downturns.

Another major concern is the lack of benefits and protections for gig workers. Traditional employees typically receive benefits such as health insurance, paid leave, and retirement plans, which provide important support and security. In contrast, gig workers are often classified as independent contractors, meaning they are not entitled to these benefits. This classification can leave gig workers without access to essential protections, such as unemployment insurance, workers' compensation, and health coverage. As a result, gig workers may face significant financial and personal risks, particularly in the event of illness, injury, or job loss.

The gig economy also raises questions about workers' rights and labor standards. The classification of gig workers as independent contractors means they are not covered by many labor laws that protect traditional employees. For example, minimum wage laws, overtime regulations, and anti-discrimination protections may not apply to gig workers, leaving them vulnerable to exploitation and unfair treatment. This lack of legal protection has sparked debates about the need to update labor laws to better reflect the realities of the gig economy and ensure fair treatment for all workers.

Despite these challenges, the gig economy continues to grow and evolve, driven by advances in technology and changing attitudes towards work. As digital platforms become more sophisticated, they offer new opportunities for innovation and efficiency. For example, artificial intelligence and machine learning can enhance gig platforms by better matching workers with gigs that suit their skills and preferences, improving the overall user experience. Additionally, blockchain technology can provide greater transparency and security in gig transactions, ensuring that workers are paid fairly and promptly for their services.

The gig economy is also driving changes in how businesses approach talent management and workforce planning. As companies increasingly rely on gig workers to meet their needs, they must develop strategies for effectively integrating these workers into their operations. This may involve rethinking traditional HR practices, such as recruitment, training, and performance management, to accommodate the unique characteristics of gig work. For instance, businesses may need to invest in digital tools and platforms that facilitate collaboration and communication with gig workers, ensuring that they can contribute effectively to the organization's goals.

Moreover, the gig economy is prompting a reevaluation of education and skills development. As the nature of work changes, so too must the way individuals prepare for and navigate their careers. Lifelong learning and continuous skills development are becoming increasingly important, as workers must adapt to new technologies and market demands. Educational institutions and training providers are responding to this need by offering more flexible, accessible, and relevant programs that help individuals acquire the skills necessary for success in the gig economy. For example, online courses and micro-credentials can provide targeted training in specific areas, enabling workers to quickly upskill and remain competitive in the job market.

The gig economy is also influencing the broader cultural and societal perceptions of work. Traditional notions of career success, which often emphasize long-term employment with a single employer, are being challenged by the rise of gig work. For many, success is no longer defined by job titles or tenure, but by the ability to achieve a fulfilling and balanced life through diverse work experiences. This shift in mindset is reflected in the growing popularity of portfolio careers, where individuals build a career through a combination of different gigs, projects, and roles. This approach allows for greater personal and professional growth, as workers can explore different interests and develop a wide range of skills.

As the gig economy continues to reshape the workforce landscape, policymakers and stakeholders must address the challenges and opportunities it presents. Ensuring fair treatment and protection for gig workers is essential for creating a sustainable and equitable gig economy. This may involve updating labor laws to provide gig workers with access to benefits and protections, such as health insurance, paid leave, and retirement plans. Additionally, policies that promote financial security, such as portable benefits that move with workers from gig to gig, can help mitigate the risks associated with gig work.

Collaboration between businesses, governments, and gig platforms is crucial for developing solutions that support both workers and employers. For example, gig platforms can play a role in providing benefits and protections to their workers, either directly or through partnerships with insurance providers and other service providers. Businesses can also contribute by adopting fair and transparent practices when engaging gig workers, ensuring that they are paid fairly and treated with respect.

As the gig economy continues to evolve, it is essential to monitor its impact on workers, businesses, and society as a whole. Research and data collection can provide valuable insights into the experiences and needs of gig workers, informing policy decisions and helping to develop targeted interventions. By understanding the dynamics of the gig economy, stakeholders can create an environment that supports innovation and growth while ensuring that gig workers are treated fairly and have access to the benefits and protections they need.

The gig economy represents a fundamental shift in the way people work and businesses operate. Its rise is driven by the desire for flexibility, autonomy, and efficiency, offering significant advantages for both workers and employers. However, it also presents challenges related to job security, benefits, and workers' rights that must be addressed to create a sustainable and equitable future of work. By embracing the opportunities and addressing the challenges of the gig economy, we can build a workforce landscape that is dynamic, inclusive, and resilient, ultimately benefiting workers, businesses, and society as a whole.

ᗖᗖᗖ

*"Blockchain offers a new paradigm of trust and transparency in business. By decentralizing data, we can create more secure and equitable systems. Let's harness blockchain to build a foundation of integrity in the digital age."*

# FIVE

# REMOTE WORK REVOLUTION - THE FUTURE OF THE WORKPLACE

The remote work revolution has fundamentally transformed the landscape of the modern workplace, altering how businesses operate and how employees perform their tasks. While remote work was already gaining traction due to advancements in technology and changing attitudes toward work-life balance, the COVID-19 pandemic accelerated its adoption on a global scale. As companies and workers adapted to this new reality, it became clear that remote work is not merely a temporary solution but a permanent shift that will shape the future of work. This transformation has profound implications for productivity, employee well-being, corporate culture, and the design of work itself.

Remote work is powered by a suite of digital tools and technologies that enable employees to perform their duties from virtually anywhere. High-speed internet, cloud computing, collaboration software, and virtual communication platforms like Zoom,

Microsoft Teams, and Slack have become essential components of the remote work infrastructure. These technologies facilitate seamless communication, collaboration, and access to information, allowing teams to work together effectively despite geographical distances. The ability to share documents in real-time, conduct virtual meetings, and manage projects online has made remote work not only possible but also efficient and productive.

One of the most significant benefits of remote work is the flexibility it offers employees. Without the constraints of a traditional office environment, workers can design their schedules around their personal lives, leading to improved work-life balance. This flexibility can reduce stress and increase job satisfaction, as employees have more control over their time and can better accommodate personal responsibilities and interests. For instance, a parent working remotely can adjust their work hours to attend to their children's needs, while an employee with a long commute can eliminate travel time, freeing up more time for work and leisure activities. This autonomy can result in higher morale and greater employee retention, as workers feel more empowered and valued.

For businesses, remote work presents an opportunity to tap into a global talent pool. Companies are no longer limited by geographic location when hiring, enabling them to find the best talent regardless of where they are based. This expanded access to diverse skills and perspectives can drive innovation and enhance competitiveness. Moreover, remote work can lead to cost savings by reducing the need for physical office space, utilities, and other overhead expenses associated with maintaining a traditional office. Businesses can reallocate these savings toward other strategic initiatives, such as employee development, technology investments, and customer engagement.

Productivity is a key concern for both employers and employees when it comes to remote work. Contrary to initial fears, studies have shown that remote work can enhance productivity. Without the distractions and interruptions of a typical office environment, many employees find they can focus better and accomplish more. Additionally, the flexibility to work during their most productive hours can lead to higher output and efficiency. However, this increased productivity often requires effective time management skills and self-discipline, as the home environment can present its own set of distractions. Employers can support their remote workforce by providing training on best practices for remote work, setting clear expectations, and encouraging regular breaks to prevent burnout.

While remote work offers numerous advantages, it also poses challenges that must be addressed to ensure its long-term success. One significant challenge is maintaining communication and collaboration among team members who are not physically co-located. Virtual communication tools can bridge this gap, but they cannot fully replicate the spontaneity and richness of in-person interactions. To foster effective communication, companies need to establish clear protocols and use a variety of communication channels to cater to different needs. Regular virtual meetings, team-building activities, and social interactions can help maintain a sense of connection and camaraderie among remote workers.

Another challenge is preserving corporate culture in a remote work environment. Corporate culture is often built through shared experiences, informal interactions, and the physical presence of team members. Remote work can dilute these elements, making it harder to instill a strong sense of identity and belonging. To address this, companies must be intentional about nurturing their culture remotely. This can involve creating virtual spaces for casual conversations, celebrating achievements and milestones online, and reinforcing company values through regular communication. Leadership plays a crucial role in modeling and promoting the desired culture, ensuring that it permeates throughout the organization despite the physical distance.

Employee well-being is another critical consideration in the remote work revolution. While remote work can enhance work-life balance, it can also blur the boundaries between work and personal life, leading to overwork and burnout. Without the clear separation provided by a physical office, employees may struggle to disconnect from work, leading to increased stress and decreased mental health. Employers can support their remote workforce by encouraging healthy work habits, such as setting boundaries, taking regular breaks, and maintaining a consistent schedule. Providing access to mental health resources, promoting wellness programs, and fostering an open dialogue about well-being can also help mitigate the risks associated with remote work.

The physical workspace at home is another important aspect of remote work. Not all employees have access to a dedicated home office or ergonomic furniture, which can impact their comfort and productivity. Employers can support their remote workers by offering stipends or resources to create a conducive work environment at home. This might include providing ergonomic chairs, standing desks, or other office supplies that enhance comfort and reduce the risk of physical strain. Additionally, educating employees on the importance of ergonomics and proper workspace setup can contribute to a healthier and more productive remote work experience.

Security and data privacy are critical considerations in a remote work setup. With employees accessing company systems and data from various locations, the risk of security breaches and cyberattacks increases. Companies must implement robust security measures to protect sensitive information and ensure compliance with data protection regulations. This can involve using virtual private networks (VPNs), multi-factor authentication, and encryption to secure communications and data. Providing regular training on cybersecurity best practices and encouraging vigilance can help employees recognize and respond to potential threats.

The remote work revolution also has implications for urban planning and real estate. As more companies adopt remote work policies, the demand for office space may decline, leading to changes in commercial real estate markets. Cities may see a shift in how office spaces are used, with some being repurposed for residential or mixed-use developments. Additionally, the reduced need for commuting can decrease traffic congestion and lower carbon emissions, contributing to more sustainable urban environments. However, this shift may also impact local businesses that rely on office workers, such as restaurants, cafes, and retail stores. Urban planners and policymakers will need to consider these changes and adapt their strategies to support the evolving needs of their communities.

Education and professional development are also being transformed by the remote work revolution. As remote work becomes more prevalent, the demand for digital skills and remote work competencies increases. Educational institutions and training providers must adapt their curricula to prepare students for the future of work, emphasizing skills such as digital literacy, remote collaboration, and self-management. Additionally, companies must invest in ongoing training and development programs to ensure their employees remain competitive and equipped to thrive in a remote work environment. Online learning platforms and virtual training programs can provide accessible and flexible options for skill development, enabling employees to continue their education while balancing work and personal commitments.

Leadership and management practices must also evolve to support remote work. Traditional management approaches that rely on direct supervision and physical presence may not be effective in a remote setting. Leaders must develop new strategies for managing remote teams, focusing on outcomes rather than activities. This involves setting clear goals, providing regular feedback, and empowering employees to take ownership of their work. Building trust is essential, as remote work requires a high degree of autonomy and self-direction. Leaders can foster trust by being transparent, consistent, and supportive, creating an environment where employees feel valued and respected.

Performance evaluation and career advancement are areas that require careful consideration in a remote work context. Traditional performance metrics that focus on hours worked or physical presence may not be relevant or fair for remote workers. Instead, companies should adopt outcome-based evaluation methods that assess performance based on results and contributions. This approach ensures that employees are recognized and rewarded for their achievements, regardless of where they work. Additionally, companies must provide opportunities for remote workers to advance their careers, offering pathways for growth and development that are accessible to all employees, whether they are in the office or working remotely.

The remote work revolution is not without its critics, who argue that it may lead to social isolation and a lack of team cohesion. While these concerns are valid, they can be addressed through thoughtful and intentional practices. Companies can create opportunities for social interaction and team building, both virtually and in person, to maintain strong relationships and a sense of community. Hybrid work models, which combine remote and in-office work, can offer a balance that meets the needs of both employees and employers. By allowing for flexibility while maintaining some level of physical presence, hybrid models can provide the best of both worlds, fostering collaboration and connection while supporting individual preferences and circumstances.

The future of work is undoubtedly shaped by the remote work revolution, and its impact will continue to unfold in the coming years. As companies and employees navigate this new landscape, they will need to remain adaptable and open to change. The lessons learned during the rapid shift to remote work during the pandemic will inform future practices and policies, driving innovation and improvement. By embracing the opportunities and addressing the challenges of remote work, businesses can create a more flexible, inclusive, and resilient workforce that is well-equipped to thrive in the digital age.

Ultimately, the remote work revolution represents a significant shift in how we think about work and its role in our lives. It challenges traditional notions of the workplace and offers a vision of a more flexible and dynamic future. As we move forward, it is essential to continue exploring new ways to support and empower remote workers, ensuring that the benefits of this transformation are realized for all. By doing so, we can build a future of work that is not only more productive and efficient but also more fulfilling and balanced for everyone involved.

ᛏᛏᛏ

"The gig economy redefines flexibility and opportunity in the workforce. However, we must ensure that it also provides security and fairness. A balanced approach will unlock its full potential for both workers and businesses."

# SIX

# SUSTAINABILITY AND GREEN BUSINESS - ECO-FRIENDLY PRACTICES FOR GROWTH

Sustainability and green business practices have become central themes in the contemporary corporate landscape as organizations increasingly recognize the importance of environmental stewardship for long-term growth. The need for sustainable development arises from the pressing global challenges of climate change, resource depletion, and environmental degradation. Businesses across various industries are responding by integrating eco-friendly practices into their operations, thereby contributing to a more sustainable future while also reaping economic and reputational benefits.

At the heart of green business practices is the concept of sustainability, which emphasizes the need to meet present needs without compromising the ability of future generations to meet theirs. This involves a holistic approach to business operations that considers environmental, social, and economic impacts. Companies are adopting strategies that reduce their carbon footprint, conserve natural resources, and promote social equity. By doing so, they not only contribute to environmental preservation but also build resilience against regulatory pressures, market fluctuations, and stakeholder expectations.

One of the most significant ways businesses can embrace sustainability is by reducing their carbon emissions. The increasing concentration of greenhouse gases in the atmosphere, primarily due to human activities, is a major driver of climate change. Businesses can mitigate their impact by adopting energy-efficient technologies, transitioning to renewable energy sources, and optimizing their supply chains. For instance, companies can invest in solar panels, wind turbines, or geothermal energy to power their operations. Additionally, enhancing energy efficiency through the use of LED lighting, smart thermostats, and energy management systems can significantly lower energy consumption and costs.

Supply chain management plays a crucial role in a company's sustainability efforts. A sustainable supply chain minimizes environmental impact at every stage, from sourcing raw materials to product disposal. Companies can achieve this by partnering with suppliers who adhere to environmentally friendly practices, using recycled or sustainable materials, and implementing circular economy principles. The circular economy emphasizes reducing waste by keeping products and materials in use for as long as possible through recycling, reusing, and refurbishing. For example, a company might design products that are easier to disassemble and recycle, or it might offer take-back programs to manage product end-of-life responsibly.

Water conservation is another critical aspect of sustainable business practices. Water is a finite resource, and many regions around the world are facing water scarcity due to over-extraction and climate change. Businesses can reduce their water footprint by implementing efficient water management practices, such as using water-saving technologies, recycling wastewater, and adopting sustainable agricultural practices. For example, companies in the food and beverage industry can invest in drip irrigation systems that deliver water directly to plant roots, reducing water use and increasing efficiency. Additionally, industries can treat and reuse wastewater in their processes, minimizing the need for fresh water and reducing pollution.

Waste reduction is a fundamental component of green business practices. By minimizing waste, companies can lower their environmental impact, reduce costs, and improve operational efficiency. Businesses can achieve this by implementing waste reduction strategies, such as reducing packaging, increasing recycling, and composting organic waste. For instance, retailers can reduce packaging waste by using minimal, recyclable, or biodegradable materials. Manufacturing companies can adopt lean manufacturing principles to minimize waste during production processes. Additionally, food companies can partner with organizations to donate surplus food, reducing food waste and supporting communities in need.

Green building practices are essential for reducing the environmental impact of construction and operation of buildings. Sustainable buildings are designed to be energy-efficient, water-efficient, and environmentally friendly throughout their lifecycle. This includes the use of sustainable materials, energy-efficient systems, and design principles that enhance natural lighting and ventilation. Certifications such as LEED (Leadership in Energy and Environmental Design) provide frameworks for constructing and operating green buildings. Companies can achieve LEED certification by incorporating elements such as energy-efficient HVAC systems, low-emission materials, and green roofs that provide insulation and reduce urban heat island effects.

Sustainable transportation practices are also crucial for reducing a company's carbon footprint. Transportation is a major contributor to greenhouse gas emissions, and businesses can adopt eco-friendly transportation strategies to mitigate their impact. This includes transitioning to electric or hybrid vehicles, optimizing logistics to reduce travel distances, and encouraging alternative modes of transportation such as cycling and public transit. For example, a delivery company can switch to electric delivery vans and implement route optimization software to reduce fuel consumption and emissions. Additionally, companies can incentivize employees to use public transportation or carpool through commuter benefits programs.

Corporate social responsibility (CSR) initiatives are integral to a company's sustainability strategy. CSR encompasses a company's efforts to contribute positively to society and the environment beyond its core business operations. This includes philanthropic activities, community engagement, and initiatives that promote social equity. For instance, a company might support reforestation projects, invest in renewable energy research, or partner with local organizations to address social issues such as poverty and education. By engaging in CSR activities, companies can enhance their reputation, build stronger relationships with stakeholders, and contribute to the overall well-being of society.

Sustainability reporting is a key practice for companies committed to transparency and accountability in their environmental and social impacts. Sustainability reports provide stakeholders with information on a company's sustainability goals, initiatives, and performance. These reports often follow established frameworks such as the Global Reporting Initiative (GRI) or the Sustainability Accounting Standards Board (SASB), which provide guidelines for measuring and reporting on sustainability metrics. By publishing sustainability reports, companies can demonstrate their commitment to sustainability, build trust with stakeholders, and identify areas for improvement.

Employee engagement is critical to the success of sustainability initiatives. Companies can foster a culture of sustainability by educating and empowering employees to adopt eco-friendly practices in their work and personal lives. This can include training programs, sustainability workshops, and incentive programs that reward employees for contributing to sustainability goals. For example, a company might implement a green office program that encourages employees to reduce energy use, recycle, and participate in carpooling. By involving employees in sustainability efforts, companies can harness their creativity and enthusiasm to drive positive change.

Innovation and technology play pivotal roles in advancing sustainability. Businesses can leverage cutting-edge technologies to develop sustainable products, optimize processes, and reduce environmental impact. For instance, advancements in material science can lead to the creation of biodegradable plastics and sustainable packaging solutions. Renewable energy technologies, such as advanced solar panels and energy storage systems, can enhance energy efficiency and reduce reliance on fossil fuels. Additionally, digital technologies such as the Internet of Things (IoT) and artificial intelligence (AI) can optimize resource use, monitor environmental impact, and improve decision-making. For example, IoT sensors can track energy and water use in real-time, enabling businesses to identify inefficiencies and make data-driven adjustments.

Collaboration and partnerships are essential for achieving

sustainability goals. No single organization can address global environmental challenges alone, and businesses can benefit from working together with other companies, governments, non-governmental organizations (NGOs), and communities. Collaborative efforts can include joint ventures, industry coalitions, and public-private partnerships that focus on sustainability initiatives. For example, companies in the fashion industry might collaborate to develop sustainable supply chains and reduce the environmental impact of textile production. By sharing knowledge, resources, and best practices, businesses can amplify their impact and drive systemic change.

Consumer demand for sustainable products and practices is a powerful driver of green business. Increasingly, consumers are making purchasing decisions based on a company's environmental and social performance. Companies that adopt sustainable practices can attract environmentally conscious consumers, differentiate themselves in the market, and build brand loyalty. For instance, a company that offers organic, ethically sourced products can appeal to consumers who prioritize sustainability in their purchasing decisions. Additionally, transparent communication about sustainability efforts can build consumer trust and enhance a company's reputation.

The regulatory environment is another important factor influencing the adoption of sustainable practices. Governments around the world are implementing policies and regulations to address environmental issues and promote sustainability. These regulations can include emissions targets, renewable energy mandates, and waste reduction requirements. Companies must stay informed about regulatory developments and ensure compliance to avoid penalties and enhance their competitive advantage. Proactive engagement with policymakers and participation in the regulatory process can also help businesses shape the future regulatory landscape and advocate for policies that support sustainable development.

The financial sector is increasingly recognizing the importance of sustainability in investment decisions. Sustainable investing, also known as responsible or ESG (environmental, social, and governance) investing, integrates sustainability considerations into investment strategies. Investors are looking for companies that demonstrate strong sustainability performance, as these companies are often better positioned to manage risks and capitalize on opportunities. By prioritizing sustainability, businesses can attract investment from ESG-focused funds and enhance their long-term financial performance. Additionally, companies can issue green bonds to finance sustainability projects, providing investors with opportunities to support environmentally beneficial initiatives.

Education and awareness are critical for advancing sustainability. Businesses can play a role in educating consumers, employees, and other stakeholders about the importance of sustainable practices. This can include marketing campaigns, sustainability reports, and community outreach programs that highlight the company's sustainability efforts and encourage others to take action. By raising awareness and promoting sustainable behaviors, businesses can contribute to a broader cultural shift towards environmental responsibility.

The journey towards sustainability is an ongoing process that requires continuous improvement and adaptation. Companies must regularly assess their sustainability performance, set ambitious goals, and seek opportunities for innovation and improvement. This can involve conducting environmental impact assessments, benchmarking against industry standards, and engaging with stakeholders to gather feedback and insights. By fostering a culture of continuous improvement, businesses can stay ahead of evolving environmental challenges and drive meaningful progress towards a sustainable future.

In conclusion, sustainability and green business practices are essential for addressing global environmental challenges and ensuring long-term growth. By adopting eco-friendly practices, businesses can reduce their environmental impact, build resilience, and enhance their competitive advantage. This holistic approach to sustainability encompasses a wide range of strategies, from reducing carbon emissions and conserving water to promoting social equity and fostering innovation. As companies, consumers, and policymakers increasingly prioritize sustainability, businesses that embrace these practices will be well-positioned to thrive in a rapidly changing world. Through collaboration, innovation, and a commitment to continuous improvement, the corporate sector can play a pivotal role in creating a more sustainable and prosperous future for all.

ႃႃႃ

"Remote work is more than a trend; it's a shift towards a more flexible and inclusive work environment. To succeed, businesses must foster engagement and support well-being. Embrace the future of work with empathy and adaptability."

# SEVEN

# E-COMMERCE EVOLUTION – ADAPTING TO NEW CONSUMER BEHAVIORS

The evolution of e-commerce has profoundly transformed the retail landscape, reshaping how consumers shop and businesses operate. As technology advances and consumer behaviors shift, e-commerce continues to adapt, driving innovation and redefining the shopping experience. This transformation is characterized by the integration of advanced technologies, changes in consumer expectations, and the emergence of new business models. Understanding these dynamics is crucial for businesses seeking to thrive in the digital marketplace.

The rise of e-commerce can be traced back to the late 20th century with the advent of the internet. Early online retailers, such as Amazon and eBay, capitalized on the internet's potential to reach a global audience, offering consumers unprecedented convenience and access to a wide range of products. Over the years, e-commerce has evolved from simple online storefronts to sophisticated platforms that leverage data analytics, artificial intelligence, and other advanced technologies to enhance the shopping experience.

One of the most significant drivers of e-commerce evolution is the rapid advancement of technology. High-speed internet, mobile devices, and secure payment systems have made online shopping more accessible and convenient. Mobile commerce, or m-commerce, has seen explosive growth, with consumers increasingly using smartphones and tablets to browse and purchase products. This shift has prompted businesses to optimize their websites and applications for mobile devices, ensuring a seamless and user-friendly experience.

Artificial intelligence (AI) and machine learning (ML) are at the forefront of e-commerce innovation, transforming how businesses interact with consumers. AI-powered chatbots and virtual assistants provide personalized customer service, answering queries and guiding shoppers through the purchasing process. These technologies enhance customer engagement by offering real-time assistance and tailored recommendations based on individual preferences and browsing history. Additionally, AI-driven algorithms analyze vast amounts of data to predict consumer behavior, optimize pricing strategies, and manage inventory more effectively.

Personalization is a key trend in the evolution of e-commerce, driven by consumers' desire for tailored experiences. Businesses use data analytics to gather insights into consumer preferences, purchase history, and browsing behavior, enabling them to deliver personalized product recommendations and marketing messages. This level of customization enhances customer satisfaction and loyalty, as shoppers feel understood and valued. For example, streaming services like Netflix and music platforms like Spotify use AI to recommend content based on users' past interactions, creating a more engaging experience.

The integration of augmented reality (AR) and virtual reality (VR) into e-commerce is another significant development. These technologies offer immersive shopping experiences that bridge the gap between online and offline retail. AR allows consumers to visualize products in their own environment before making a purchase. For instance, furniture retailers like IKEA offer AR apps that enable shoppers to see how a piece of furniture would look in their home. VR creates virtual stores where customers can explore products in a simulated environment, enhancing the online shopping experience with a sense of presence and interactivity.

Social media has also played a pivotal role in the evolution of e-commerce, giving rise to social commerce. Platforms like Instagram, Facebook, and Pinterest have integrated shopping features that allow users to discover and purchase products directly through social media. Influencer marketing and user-generated content further drive social commerce, as consumers increasingly rely on recommendations from their social networks and favorite influencers. This trend highlights the importance of building a strong social media presence and engaging with consumers on these platforms to drive sales and brand loyalty.

Subscription-based models have gained popularity in e-commerce, offering consumers convenience and value. Subscription services provide regular deliveries of products, such as beauty boxes, meal kits, and pet supplies, tailored to individual preferences. This model fosters customer retention and predictable revenue streams for businesses. Additionally, subscription services often create a sense of community and exclusivity, enhancing customer loyalty and engagement. Companies like Birchbox and Dollar Shave Club have successfully leveraged subscription models to build strong, loyal customer bases.

The evolution of e-commerce has also led to the emergence of direct-to-consumer (DTC) brands, which bypass traditional retail channels to sell products directly to customers. DTC brands leverage digital platforms to reach their target audience, build brand identity, and collect valuable customer data. This approach allows for greater control over the customer experience and fosters a direct relationship with consumers. Brands like Warby Parker and Glossier have disrupted traditional retail by offering high-quality products at competitive prices through their online platforms, creating loyal followings and strong brand recognition.

Sustainability has become a crucial consideration for consumers, influencing their purchasing decisions and shaping e-commerce trends. Eco-conscious shoppers seek products that align with their values, prioritizing sustainable practices, ethical sourcing, and minimal environmental impact. Businesses are responding by adopting green practices, such as using eco-friendly packaging, offering carbon-neutral shipping options, and sourcing materials responsibly. Transparency and authenticity are essential in communicating these efforts, as consumers increasingly demand accountability and proof of sustainability claims.

The COVID-19 pandemic accelerated the shift towards e-commerce, as lockdowns and social distancing measures forced consumers to turn to online shopping. This sudden surge in demand highlighted the importance of having a robust online presence and the ability to scale operations quickly. Businesses that had already invested in e-commerce infrastructure were better positioned to navigate the challenges, while others had to rapidly adapt to meet the new consumer expectations. The pandemic underscored the need for resilience and flexibility in the face of unforeseen disruptions, driving further innovation and investment in e-commerce capabilities.

Logistics and supply chain management are critical components of e-commerce, directly impacting customer satisfaction and operational efficiency. The rise of e-commerce has increased the demand for fast and reliable delivery services. Companies are investing in last-mile delivery solutions, such as drone deliveries and autonomous vehicles, to expedite shipping and reduce costs. Fulfillment centers and warehouses are becoming more automated, using robotics and AI to manage inventory, pick and pack orders, and optimize workflows. Efficient logistics are essential for meeting consumer expectations for quick delivery times and seamless returns, which are key drivers of customer loyalty.

Cross-border e-commerce is expanding as consumers seek unique products and better deals from international markets. Advances in payment processing, logistics, and language translation have made it easier for businesses to reach global audiences. Companies are adapting their strategies to navigate the complexities of international trade, including currency exchange, customs regulations, and local consumer preferences. By offering localized experiences and addressing the specific needs of different markets, businesses can tap into new revenue streams and grow their global footprint.

Data security and privacy are paramount concerns in e-commerce, as businesses handle vast amounts of sensitive customer information. Protecting this data from breaches and ensuring compliance with regulations, such as the General Data Protection Regulation (GDPR), is essential for maintaining consumer trust. Companies must implement robust cybersecurity measures, including encryption, multi-factor authentication, and regular security audits. Transparency in data handling practices and clear communication of privacy policies are crucial for building and sustaining consumer confidence.

The future of e-commerce is likely to be shaped by continued technological advancements and evolving consumer behaviors. Emerging technologies, such as blockchain, 5G, and the Internet of Things (IoT), have the potential to further transform the industry. Blockchain can enhance transparency and security in transactions, supply chains, and product authenticity. 5G technology will enable faster and more reliable internet connections, improving the overall online shopping experience. IoT devices, such as smart home assistants and connected appliances, can facilitate seamless and intuitive shopping experiences, from voice-activated orders to automated reordering of household supplies.

Artificial intelligence and machine learning will continue to play a significant role in enhancing e-commerce. These technologies will drive further personalization, enabling businesses to deliver highly targeted marketing messages and product recommendations. Predictive analytics will help companies anticipate consumer demand, optimize inventory levels, and reduce waste. AI-powered chatbots and virtual assistants will become even more sophisticated, providing real-time, context-aware customer support. As AI and ML technologies evolve, they will unlock new possibilities for enhancing the customer experience and driving business growth.

Sustainability will remain a critical focus for e-commerce, with consumers demanding greater accountability and transparency from businesses. Companies will need to innovate in areas such as packaging, supply chain management, and product design to meet sustainability goals. Circular economy principles will gain traction, with businesses exploring ways to extend product lifecycles through recycling, refurbishment, and reuse. Consumers will increasingly prioritize brands that demonstrate genuine commitment to environmental and social responsibility.

The integration of physical and digital retail experiences, known as omnichannel retailing, will become more seamless and sophisticated. Consumers expect a consistent and cohesive experience across all touchpoints, whether they are shopping online, in-store, or through a mobile app. Businesses will invest in technologies that enable seamless transitions between channels, such as integrated inventory systems, unified customer profiles, and consistent branding. Click-and-collect services, where customers order online and pick up in-store, will continue to grow in popularity, offering convenience and flexibility.

As e-commerce evolves, the importance of customer experience cannot be overstated. In a highly competitive market, businesses must differentiate themselves by providing exceptional and memorable experiences. This involves not only meeting but exceeding customer expectations at every touchpoint. From intuitive website design and efficient checkout processes to responsive customer service and hassle-free returns, every aspect of the customer journey matters. Businesses that prioritize customer experience will build loyal customer bases, drive repeat business, and generate positive word-of-mouth.

The evolution of e-commerce is a dynamic and ongoing process, driven by technological innovation, changing consumer behaviors, and market forces. As businesses navigate this landscape, they must remain agile, customer-centric, and forward-thinking. Embracing new technologies, adapting to shifting consumer preferences, and prioritizing sustainability will be key to success in the digital marketplace. By staying attuned to trends and continuously innovating, businesses can harness the full potential of e-commerce to drive growth and create lasting value for their customers. The future of e-commerce holds immense promise, and those who adapt and evolve will be well-positioned to thrive in this ever-changing environment.

ᑭᑭᑭ

"Sustainability is not a choice but a necessity for businesses today. Integrating eco-friendly practices is essential for long-term success and planetary health. Let's commit to green business practices that drive both profit and progress."

# EIGHT

# Fintech Innovations – Disrupting Traditional Finance Models

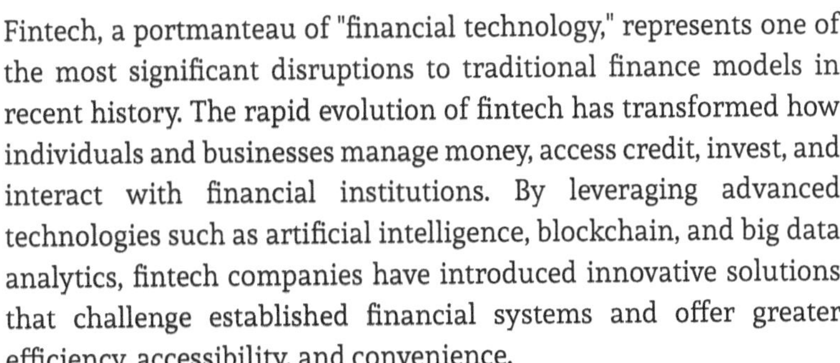

Fintech, a portmanteau of "financial technology," represents one of the most significant disruptions to traditional finance models in recent history. The rapid evolution of fintech has transformed how individuals and businesses manage money, access credit, invest, and interact with financial institutions. By leveraging advanced technologies such as artificial intelligence, blockchain, and big data analytics, fintech companies have introduced innovative solutions that challenge established financial systems and offer greater efficiency, accessibility, and convenience.

At the heart of fintech's disruption is the democratization of financial services. Traditional financial institutions, such as banks and credit unions, have long held a monopoly on financial services, often characterized by complex processes, high fees, and limited accessibility. Fintech companies, on the other hand, aim to make financial services more inclusive and user-friendly. By utilizing digital platforms, fintech firms can reach a broader audience, including underserved populations who may not have access to traditional banking services. Mobile banking apps, for example, allow users to open accounts, transfer money, and pay bills without needing to visit a physical branch, thus providing financial services to individuals in remote or rural areas.

One of the most transformative aspects of fintech is its impact on payments and transactions. Digital payment systems, such as PayPal, Venmo, and Square, have revolutionized the way people send and receive money. These platforms offer a seamless and secure way to conduct transactions, whether for personal transfers, online shopping, or business payments. The convenience and speed of digital payments have made them increasingly popular, reducing the reliance on cash and traditional banking methods. Additionally, mobile payment solutions like Apple Pay and Google Wallet have further streamlined the payment process by allowing users to make purchases with a simple tap of their smartphones.

Peer-to-peer (P2P) lending is another area where fintech has significantly disrupted traditional finance. P2P lending platforms, such as LendingClub and Prosper, connect borrowers directly with lenders, bypassing traditional banks. This model offers several advantages: borrowers can often secure loans at lower interest rates than those offered by banks, while lenders can achieve higher returns on their investments compared to traditional savings accounts. By eliminating intermediaries, P2P lending platforms reduce costs and increase efficiency, making borrowing and lending more accessible to a wider audience.

Robo-advisors are another fintech innovation that has democratized access to investment services. Traditional financial advisory services often come with high fees and minimum investment requirements, making them inaccessible to many individuals. Robo-advisors, such as Betterment and Wealthfront, use algorithms and machine learning to provide automated, personalized investment advice at a fraction of the cost. These platforms analyze users' financial goals, risk tolerance, and time horizon to create and manage diversified investment portfolios. The low fees and accessibility of robo-advisors have attracted a new generation of investors, many of whom may have previously been excluded from traditional investment services.

Blockchain technology, the underlying technology behind cryptocurrencies like Bitcoin, is another groundbreaking innovation in the fintech space. Blockchain is a decentralized ledger that records transactions across a network of computers in a secure and transparent manner. This technology has the potential to revolutionize various aspects of finance, including payments, clearing and settlement, and identity verification. For instance, blockchain can enable faster and more secure cross-border payments by eliminating the need for intermediaries and reducing transaction costs. Additionally, blockchain's transparency and immutability make it an ideal solution for preventing fraud and ensuring the integrity of financial transactions.

Cryptocurrencies themselves represent a significant departure from traditional financial models. Bitcoin, the first and most well-known cryptocurrency, was created as a decentralized digital currency that operates independently of any central authority. Since its inception, numerous other cryptocurrencies, such as Ethereum, Ripple, and Litecoin, have emerged, each offering unique features and use cases. Cryptocurrencies have gained traction as an alternative asset class, attracting investors seeking diversification and potential high returns. However, their volatility and regulatory uncertainty pose challenges that continue to shape the evolving landscape of digital currencies.

Insurtech, a subset of fintech, focuses on disrupting the insurance industry through technology. Traditional insurance processes can be cumbersome and opaque, often involving lengthy paperwork and complex underwriting procedures. Insurtech companies, such as Lemonade and Root, aim to simplify and streamline these processes using artificial intelligence, data analytics, and digital platforms. For example, AI-powered chatbots can handle customer inquiries and claims processing, reducing the need for human intervention and speeding up the resolution process. Additionally, insurtech firms use data analytics to assess risk more accurately and offer personalized insurance products tailored to individual needs.

Regtech, another subset of fintech, addresses the challenges of regulatory compliance in the financial industry. Regulatory compliance is a critical and often resource-intensive aspect of financial services, as institutions must adhere to various laws and regulations to prevent fraud, money laundering, and other illicit activities. Regtech companies leverage technology to automate compliance processes, reduce costs, and enhance the accuracy of regulatory reporting. For instance, machine learning algorithms can analyze large volumes of transaction data to detect suspicious activities and generate real-time alerts for compliance officers. By improving the efficiency and effectiveness of compliance efforts, regtech solutions help financial institutions navigate the complex regulatory landscape.

The rise of fintech has also spurred the growth of digital-only banks, also known as neobanks. Unlike traditional banks with physical branches, neobanks operate entirely online, offering a wide range of banking services through mobile apps and websites. Examples of neobanks include Chime, N26, and Monzo. These digital banks offer features such as fee-free accounts, high-yield savings, and advanced budgeting tools, appealing to tech-savvy consumers seeking convenience and cost savings. The streamlined operations of neobanks allow them to pass on cost savings to customers in the form of lower fees and higher interest rates, further challenging the traditional banking model.

Open banking is another fintech innovation that promotes greater competition and collaboration within the financial industry. Open banking initiatives, such as those mandated by the European Union's Revised Payment Services Directive (PSD2), require banks to share customer data with third-party providers through secure APIs (application programming interfaces). This allows fintech companies to develop innovative financial products and services that integrate seamlessly with existing bank accounts. For example, third-party apps can aggregate financial information from multiple accounts, providing users with a comprehensive view of their finances and personalized recommendations. Open banking fosters innovation and empowers consumers with greater control over their financial data.

The integration of fintech solutions into traditional financial institutions, often referred to as "fintegration," is another important trend. Recognizing the disruptive potential of fintech, many established banks and financial firms are partnering with fintech startups or developing their own digital solutions to stay competitive. These collaborations enable traditional institutions to leverage fintech innovations while maintaining their established customer base and regulatory expertise. For example, banks might integrate AI-driven fraud detection systems or offer digital wallets and payment solutions developed by fintech partners. By embracing fintech, traditional institutions can enhance their service offerings and improve customer experiences.

Despite the numerous benefits and innovations brought by fintech, the industry also faces significant challenges and risks. Cybersecurity is a critical concern, as the increasing digitization of financial services makes them vulnerable to cyberattacks and data breaches. Fintech companies must invest in robust security measures, including encryption, multi-factor authentication, and regular security audits, to protect sensitive customer information and maintain trust.

Regulatory compliance is another challenge, as fintech firms must navigate a complex and evolving regulatory landscape. Regulators are working to balance the promotion of innovation with the need to protect consumers and ensure the stability of the financial system. Fintech companies must stay informed about regulatory changes and work closely with regulators to ensure compliance. The development of regulatory sandboxes, which allow fintech firms to test new products and services in a controlled environment, is one approach that has been adopted to foster innovation while managing risks.

Financial inclusion remains a key goal for the fintech industry. While fintech has the potential to reach underserved populations, there are still barriers to access, such as limited internet connectivity, low digital literacy, and regulatory restrictions. Fintech companies must continue to develop solutions that address these barriers and work towards greater financial inclusion. This includes offering affordable and accessible financial products, providing education and support to help users navigate digital platforms, and advocating for regulatory frameworks that support innovation and inclusion.

The rapid pace of fintech innovation also raises questions about the future of work in the financial industry. As automation and AI take on more tasks traditionally performed by humans, there is a growing need for workers to acquire new skills and adapt to changing roles. Financial institutions must invest in reskilling and upskilling their workforce to prepare for the digital future. Additionally, collaboration between fintech companies and traditional financial institutions can create new opportunities for job growth and career development.

The future of fintech holds immense promise, with continued advancements in technology and growing consumer adoption driving further innovation. Emerging technologies, such as quantum computing, decentralized finance (DeFi), and digital identity solutions, have the potential to further transform the financial landscape. Quantum computing could revolutionize data processing and security, enabling faster and more secure financial transactions. DeFi, built on blockchain technology, aims to create an open and decentralized financial system that operates independently of traditional intermediaries. Digital identity solutions can enhance security and streamline onboarding processes, making it easier for individuals to access financial services.

As fintech continues to evolve, the collaboration between fintech companies, traditional financial institutions, regulators, and other stakeholders will be crucial in shaping the future of finance. By working together, these entities can ensure that fintech innovations are developed and implemented in a way that promotes financial inclusion, enhances security, and drives economic growth. The ongoing dialogue and cooperation between industry players and regulators will be essential in addressing challenges and mitigating risks, while fostering an environment that supports innovation and competition.

In conclusion, fintech innovations are fundamentally disrupting traditional finance models, offering new opportunities for efficiency, accessibility, and convenience. From digital payments and P2P lending to robo-advisors and blockchain, fintech is transforming the way individuals and businesses manage money and interact with financial services. While challenges such as cybersecurity, regulatory compliance, and financial inclusion remain, the potential benefits of fintech are immense. By embracing innovation and fostering collaboration, the financial industry can navigate the evolving landscape and create a more inclusive, secure, and efficient financial system for the future. The ongoing evolution of fintech promises to continue reshaping the financial industry, driving growth and enhancing the way we manage and experience financial services.

ϷϷϷ

"E-commerce evolution hinges on creating seamless and personalized experiences. As digital and physical retail merge, customer engagement will be key. The future of retail is about delivering convenience without compromising connection."

# NINE

# THE RISE OF BIG DATA - HARNESSING INFORMATION FOR INSIGHT

The rise of big data has fundamentally transformed the landscape of business, technology, and society. Big data refers to the vast volumes of data generated every second from various sources such as social media, sensors, digital transactions, and more. This data, characterized by its volume, velocity, and variety, holds immense potential for providing insights that can drive decision-making, innovation, and efficiency across multiple domains. Harnessing the power of big data involves sophisticated techniques for collecting, processing, analyzing, and interpreting data to extract meaningful information and actionable insights.

At the core of the big data revolution is the exponential growth in data generation. The proliferation of internet-connected devices, social media platforms, and digital transactions has led to an unprecedented surge in data production. Every click, like, share, and transaction contributes to this massive data pool. For example, social media platforms like Facebook and Twitter generate terabytes of user data daily, while e-commerce giants like Amazon record millions of transactions each day. Additionally, the advent of the Internet of Things (IoT) has further accelerated data generation, as sensors embedded in devices, vehicles, and infrastructure continuously produce streams of data.

The sheer volume of data presents both opportunities and challenges. Traditional data processing tools and techniques are often inadequate to handle the scale and complexity of big data. To address this, advanced technologies such as distributed computing, cloud storage, and parallel processing have been developed. Distributed computing frameworks like Apache Hadoop and Apache Spark allow for the processing of large datasets across clusters of computers, enabling organizations to analyze data at a scale previously unimaginable. Cloud storage solutions, provided by companies like Amazon Web Services (AWS), Google Cloud, and Microsoft Azure, offer scalable and cost-effective storage options, making it easier for businesses to manage and access their data.

Velocity, or the speed at which data is generated and processed, is another defining characteristic of big data. Real-time data processing capabilities are essential for applications that require immediate insights and actions. For example, in the financial industry, stock trading algorithms rely on real-time data to make split-second decisions. In the healthcare sector, real-time monitoring of patient vital signs through wearable devices can enable timely interventions. Technologies such as stream processing and in-memory computing are crucial for handling high-velocity data, allowing for real-time analysis and decision-making.

Variety refers to the diverse types of data that are generated, including structured, semi-structured, and unstructured data. Structured data, which is organized in rows and columns, represents a small fraction of the total data generated. Semi-structured data includes formats like JSON and XML, which contain tags and markers to separate data elements. Unstructured data, such as text, images, videos, and audio, comprises the majority of big data. Analyzing unstructured data requires advanced techniques like natural language processing (NLP), image recognition, and machine learning. These technologies enable the extraction of valuable insights from diverse data sources, enhancing the depth and breadth of analysis.

The ability to harness big data for insight hinges on sophisticated data analytics techniques. Descriptive analytics, the simplest form, involves summarizing historical data to understand what has happened. Diagnostic analytics delves deeper, exploring the reasons behind past events. Predictive analytics uses statistical models and machine learning algorithms to forecast future trends and behaviors based on historical data. Finally, prescriptive analytics goes a step further, recommending actions to achieve desired outcomes. These analytics techniques, when combined, provide a comprehensive toolkit for turning raw data into valuable insights.

One of the most transformative applications of big data is in the field of business intelligence. Companies across industries leverage big data analytics to gain a competitive edge, improve operational efficiency, and enhance customer experiences. Retailers, for example, use data from customer transactions, social media interactions, and loyalty programs to gain insights into consumer preferences and behavior. By analyzing this data, retailers can optimize inventory management, personalize marketing campaigns, and enhance customer service. E-commerce platforms like Amazon use recommendation algorithms powered by big data to suggest products based on users' browsing and purchase history, driving sales and customer satisfaction.

In the financial sector, big data analytics plays a crucial role in risk management, fraud detection, and investment strategies. Banks and financial institutions analyze transaction data, market trends, and economic indicators to assess credit risk, detect fraudulent activities, and develop investment models. High-frequency trading firms use big data to analyze market data in real-time, executing trades at lightning speed based on complex algorithms. Additionally, sentiment analysis of social media and news data helps financial analysts gauge market sentiment and make informed investment decisions.

Healthcare is another industry profoundly impacted by big data. The ability to analyze vast amounts of medical data, including electronic health records (EHRs), clinical trial data, and genomic information, has the potential to revolutionize patient care and medical research. Big data analytics enables personalized medicine, where treatments are tailored to individual patients based on their genetic makeup and health history. Predictive analytics can identify patients at risk of developing chronic conditions, allowing for early interventions and preventive care. Moreover, big data is instrumental in accelerating drug discovery and development, as researchers can analyze large datasets to identify potential drug candidates and predict their efficacy.

The transportation and logistics industry leverages big data to optimize routes, reduce fuel consumption, and improve supply chain efficiency. Fleet management systems use data from GPS devices, sensors, and traffic reports to optimize delivery routes and schedules. Predictive maintenance, enabled by big data analytics, helps identify potential equipment failures before they occur, reducing downtime and maintenance costs. Additionally, real-time tracking of shipments enhances visibility and transparency in the supply chain, improving customer satisfaction and operational efficiency.

The impact of big data extends to the public sector as well.

Governments and public agencies use big data to improve public services, enhance policy-making, and ensure public safety. Smart city initiatives rely on data from various sources, including sensors, cameras, and social media, to manage urban infrastructure, monitor traffic, and improve emergency response. Data analytics helps public health agencies track disease outbreaks, allocate resources, and design effective intervention strategies. Furthermore, big data is used to analyze crime patterns, optimize law enforcement deployment, and enhance public safety.

Education is another domain where big data is making significant strides. Educational institutions analyze data from student assessments, attendance records, and learning management systems to gain insights into student performance and learning outcomes. Predictive analytics can identify students at risk of falling behind, enabling timely interventions and personalized support. Additionally, big data helps in the development of adaptive learning platforms that tailor educational content to individual students' needs and learning styles, enhancing the overall learning experience.

Despite its transformative potential, harnessing big data for insight comes with challenges. Data privacy and security are paramount concerns, as the collection and analysis of vast amounts of personal data raise ethical and legal issues. Organizations must implement robust data protection measures, comply with regulations such as the General Data Protection Regulation (GDPR), and ensure transparency in data handling practices. Additionally, the sheer volume and complexity of big data require advanced tools and skilled professionals to manage and analyze it effectively. The shortage of data scientists and analytics experts poses a challenge for many organizations seeking to leverage big data.

Data quality is another critical challenge. Inaccurate, incomplete, or inconsistent data can lead to misleading insights and flawed decision-making. Organizations must invest in data cleaning and validation processes to ensure the accuracy and reliability of their data. Furthermore, integrating data from diverse sources, such as structured databases, unstructured text, and real-time streams, requires sophisticated data integration and management techniques.

The ethical use of big data is a growing concern. The potential for bias in data and algorithms can lead to discriminatory outcomes and reinforce existing inequalities. For example, biased data in hiring algorithms can result in unfair treatment of certain groups. Organizations must be vigilant in identifying and mitigating bias in their data and analytics processes. This includes using diverse datasets, implementing fairness checks, and involving ethicists in the design and deployment of big data solutions.

The future of big data is shaped by ongoing advancements in technology and evolving societal needs. Emerging technologies such as artificial intelligence, machine learning, and quantum computing hold the promise of unlocking new possibilities for big data analytics. AI and machine learning enable more sophisticated data analysis, uncovering patterns and insights that were previously inaccessible. Quantum computing, with its ability to perform complex calculations at unprecedented speeds, has the potential to revolutionize big data processing and analytics.

As big data continues to evolve, its applications will expand across new domains and industries. The integration of big data with emerging technologies such as the Internet of Things (IoT), 5G, and blockchain will create new opportunities for innovation and efficiency. IoT devices will generate even more data, providing real-time insights into various aspects of daily life and industrial processes. The high-speed connectivity of 5G will facilitate the seamless transfer and analysis of big data, enabling real-time applications in areas such as autonomous vehicles and smart cities.

Blockchain technology will enhance data security and transparency, ensuring the integrity of big data transactions.

In conclusion, the rise of big data represents a paradigm shift in how information is harnessed for insight and decision-making. The ability to collect, process, and analyze vast amounts of data has transformed industries, improved public services, and driven innovation. While challenges such as data privacy, security, and quality must be addressed, the potential benefits of big data are immense. By leveraging advanced technologies and adopting ethical practices, organizations can unlock the full potential of big data, driving progress and creating value in the digital age. The future of big data is bright, and its impact will continue to shape the way we live, work, and interact with the world around us.

"Big data is a powerful tool for unlocking insights and driving innovation. However, its use must be governed by ethical considerations. Responsible data practices will ensure that big data serves the greater good."

# TEN

# PERSONALIZATION AND CUSTOMER EXPERIENCE - TAILORING ENGAGEMENT STRATEGIES

Personalization and customer experience have become pivotal elements in the modern business landscape, driving the need for tailored engagement strategies that resonate with individual consumers. In an era where customers are inundated with information and choices, businesses that can offer personalized experiences stand out and build stronger, more meaningful relationships with their audience. The rise of digital technologies and big data analytics has significantly enhanced the ability of companies to understand and respond to the unique preferences and behaviors of their customers, leading to more effective engagement strategies and improved customer satisfaction.

At the core of personalization is the concept of tailoring products, services, and communications to meet the specific needs and preferences of individual customers. This approach contrasts sharply with the one-size-fits-all model that dominated traditional marketing and customer service. Personalization involves leveraging data to gain insights into customer behavior, preferences, and purchasing history. These insights allow businesses to create highly relevant and targeted interactions that enhance the customer experience.

The foundation of effective personalization lies in data collection and analysis. Modern businesses have access to vast amounts of data generated from various sources, including online transactions, social media interactions, browsing history, and customer feedback. By using advanced analytics and machine learning algorithms, companies can process this data to uncover patterns and trends that provide a deep understanding of each customer's preferences and behavior. For instance, an e-commerce platform might analyze a user's browsing and purchase history to recommend products that align with their interests, thereby increasing the likelihood of a sale.

One of the most visible applications of personalization is in digital marketing. Personalized marketing campaigns use data-driven insights to deliver targeted messages to specific segments of an audience. This can include personalized email campaigns, targeted social media ads, and customized website experiences. For example, an email marketing campaign that addresses the recipient by name and recommends products based on their previous purchases is more likely to engage the customer than a generic, mass email. Similarly, targeted ads on social media platforms can reach users based on their demographics, interests, and online behavior, making the marketing message more relevant and impactful.

Personalization also plays a crucial role in enhancing the user experience on websites and mobile apps. Personalized websites adapt their content and layout based on the user's preferences and behavior. For example, an online retailer can display personalized product recommendations on their homepage, while a news website can highlight articles that match the reader's interests. This tailored experience makes it easier for users to find what they are looking for, increasing their satisfaction and likelihood of returning to the site. Additionally, mobile apps can use personalization to offer relevant notifications, personalized content, and customized interfaces that improve the overall user experience.

Customer service is another area where personalization can have a significant impact. Personalized customer service involves recognizing and addressing the unique needs of each customer. This can be achieved through the use of customer relationship management (CRM) systems that store detailed information about each customer's interactions with the company. By accessing this information, customer service representatives can provide more informed and relevant assistance. For instance, if a customer contacts support regarding an issue with a recent purchase, the representative can quickly access the customer's order history and previous interactions, allowing them to resolve the issue more efficiently and effectively.

In addition to improving customer satisfaction, personalization can drive customer loyalty and retention. When customers feel that a company understands and values their individual preferences, they are more likely to develop a strong emotional connection with the brand. This connection fosters loyalty, as customers are more inclined to return to a brand that consistently meets their needs and expectations. Loyalty programs that offer personalized rewards and incentives based on customer behavior can further strengthen this relationship. For example, a coffee shop might offer a personalized discount on a customer's favorite drink, encouraging repeat visits and fostering a sense of appreciation.

The benefits of personalization extend beyond customer satisfaction and loyalty. Personalized engagement strategies can also lead to increased sales and revenue. By delivering relevant product recommendations and targeted marketing messages, businesses can effectively cross-sell and upsell their products. For instance, an online retailer that suggests complementary products based on a customer's purchase history can increase the average order value. Additionally, personalized promotions and discounts can drive impulse purchases and encourage customers to take advantage of limited-time offers.

Despite its numerous advantages, personalization comes with its own set of challenges. One of the primary challenges is data privacy and security. As businesses collect and analyze vast amounts of personal data, they must ensure that this data is handled responsibly and in compliance with data protection regulations. Consumers are becoming increasingly aware of their privacy rights and are concerned about how their data is being used. To build and maintain trust, businesses must be transparent about their data collection practices, provide clear privacy policies, and offer customers control over their personal information.

Another challenge is the potential for personalization to become intrusive or overwhelming. While personalized experiences can enhance customer satisfaction, overly aggressive personalization can have the opposite effect. For example, bombarding customers with too many personalized messages or recommendations can lead to fatigue and irritation. Striking the right balance between relevance and frequency is crucial for maintaining a positive customer experience. Businesses must use personalization judiciously, ensuring that it adds value without becoming a nuisance.

Achieving effective personalization also requires sophisticated technology and expertise. Implementing advanced analytics, machine learning, and AI-driven personalization systems can be complex and resource-intensive. Businesses must invest in the right tools and talent to develop and maintain these systems. Additionally, continuous monitoring and optimization are necessary to ensure that personalization efforts remain effective and aligned with evolving customer preferences. This involves regularly updating algorithms, refining data models, and testing new personalization strategies.

As technology continues to evolve, the future of personalization holds even greater promise. Emerging technologies such as artificial intelligence, machine learning, and the Internet of Things (IoT) are set to revolutionize personalization efforts. AI-powered chatbots and virtual assistants can provide real-time, personalized assistance to customers, enhancing their experience and improving efficiency. Machine learning algorithms can continuously learn from customer interactions, refining personalization efforts and delivering more accurate recommendations over time. IoT devices can collect real-time data on customer behavior and preferences, enabling even more granular and context-aware personalization.

Voice assistants, such as Amazon's Alexa and Google's Assistant, are also becoming important tools for personalized engagement. These devices can recognize individual voices and provide personalized responses based on user preferences and history. For example, a voice assistant can recommend music based on a user's listening habits or provide personalized news updates. As voice technology advances, it will become an increasingly integral part of personalized customer experiences.

Augmented reality (AR) and virtual reality (VR) are other technologies with the potential to enhance personalization. AR and VR can create immersive, personalized experiences that allow customers to interact with products in new and engaging ways.

For instance, an AR app can enable customers to visualize how furniture would look in their home, while a VR experience can provide a virtual tour of a hotel or real estate property. These technologies can help customers make more informed purchasing decisions and create memorable experiences that differentiate a brand from its competitors.

Personalization is also expected to play a crucial role in the future of customer service. Predictive analytics and AI can anticipate customer needs and proactively address issues before they arise. For example, an AI system can analyze patterns in customer interactions to identify potential problems and offer solutions preemptively. This proactive approach can enhance customer satisfaction by resolving issues quickly and efficiently. Additionally, personalized self-service options, such as AI-powered knowledge bases and interactive FAQs, can empower customers to find answers to their questions independently, reducing the need for human intervention.

The evolution of personalization will continue to be driven by advancements in data analytics and machine learning. As these technologies become more sophisticated, businesses will be able to leverage deeper insights into customer behavior and preferences. This will enable even more precise and effective personalization, resulting in highly tailored experiences that resonate with individual customers. The ability to deliver such personalized experiences will be a key differentiator for businesses in an increasingly competitive marketplace.

In conclusion, personalization and customer experience are critical components of modern engagement strategies. By leveraging data and advanced technologies, businesses can create tailored interactions that meet the unique needs and preferences of each customer. This personalized approach enhances customer satisfaction, drives loyalty, and increases sales and revenue.

However, effective personalization requires careful consideration of data privacy, technology investment, and balance to avoid intrusiveness. As technology continues to evolve, the potential for personalization to transform customer experiences will only grow, offering new opportunities for businesses to connect with their customers in meaningful and impactful ways. The future of personalization is bright, and those who embrace it will be well-positioned to thrive in the ever-changing landscape of customer engagement.

ᐅᐅᐅ

"Personalization in business is about more than just targeted marketing; it's about creating meaningful connections. By understanding our customers deeply, we can deliver value that resonates. Personalization fosters loyalty and growth."

# ELEVEN

## CYBERSECURITY IMPERATIVES - PROTECTING DIGITAL ASSETS

Cybersecurity imperatives have become a cornerstone of modern digital operations, crucial for protecting digital assets against an ever-growing array of cyber threats. As businesses and individuals increasingly rely on digital technologies for communication, commerce, and data storage, the importance of robust cybersecurity measures cannot be overstated. The stakes are high, with cyberattacks posing significant risks to financial stability, operational continuity, and reputational integrity. Understanding and addressing these imperatives involves a multifaceted approach encompassing technology, policy, and human factors.

The digital revolution has brought unprecedented convenience and efficiency, but it has also expanded the attack surface for cybercriminals. Cyber threats come in various forms, including malware, ransomware, phishing, and denial-of-service attacks. Each of these threats can have devastating consequences, from financial losses and data breaches to operational disruptions and erosion of customer trust. The increasing sophistication of cyberattacks demands equally advanced and adaptive cybersecurity strategies.

Malware, short for malicious software, encompasses a wide range of harmful programs such as viruses, worms, trojans, and spyware. These programs are designed to infiltrate and damage computer systems, steal sensitive information, or gain unauthorized access to networks. Ransomware, a specific type of malware, encrypts a victim's data and demands a ransom payment for the decryption key. High-profile ransomware attacks have crippled businesses, healthcare institutions, and government agencies, highlighting the need for robust preventive measures and effective response plans.

Phishing attacks exploit human vulnerabilities to gain access to sensitive information. Cybercriminals craft deceptive emails, messages, or websites that appear legitimate, tricking individuals into divulging passwords, credit card numbers, or other confidential data. Despite advancements in email filtering and awareness training, phishing remains a pervasive threat due to its reliance on social engineering techniques. Organizations must continuously educate their employees about recognizing and responding to phishing attempts to mitigate this risk.

Denial-of-service (DoS) and distributed denial-of-service (DDoS) attacks aim to disrupt the availability of online services by overwhelming them with traffic. These attacks can cripple websites, online services, and networks, causing significant financial and reputational damage. DDoS attacks, which involve multiple compromised systems working in concert, are particularly challenging to defend against due to their scale and complexity. Implementing robust network security measures, such as traffic filtering and rate limiting, is essential for mitigating the impact of these attacks.

Protecting digital assets requires a comprehensive approach that integrates technological defenses, policy frameworks, and human factors. Technological defenses encompass a range of tools and practices designed to detect, prevent, and respond to cyber threats. Firewalls, antivirus software, intrusion detection systems, and encryption are foundational elements of a robust cybersecurity infrastructure. These technologies work together to create multiple layers of defense, making it more difficult for cybercriminals to penetrate networks and systems.

Encryption is a critical component of cybersecurity, ensuring that sensitive data remains confidential and secure during transmission and storage. By converting data into an unreadable format, encryption prevents unauthorized access, even if the data is intercepted or stolen. Organizations must implement strong encryption protocols for all sensitive data, including communications, financial transactions, and personal information. Regularly updating encryption standards and practices is essential to stay ahead of evolving threats and vulnerabilities.

Multi-factor authentication (MFA) is another vital technology for enhancing security. MFA requires users to provide multiple forms of verification before gaining access to systems or data. This typically involves something the user knows (a password), something the user has (a smartphone or hardware token), and something the user is (biometric data such as a fingerprint). By adding an extra layer of security, MFA significantly reduces the risk of unauthorized access, even if a password is compromised.

Network security is a cornerstone of protecting digital assets. Segmentation, the practice of dividing a network into smaller, isolated segments, limits the spread of cyberattacks and minimizes potential damage. Implementing virtual private networks (VPNs) provides secure, encrypted connections for remote access, safeguarding data as it travels across public networks. Regular network monitoring and logging help detect unusual activity and potential intrusions, enabling swift response to threats.

Policy frameworks play a crucial role in establishing and enforcing cybersecurity standards. Governments and regulatory bodies have implemented various laws and regulations to ensure that organizations adopt adequate cybersecurity measures. The General Data Protection Regulation (GDPR) in the European Union, the California Consumer Privacy Act (CCPA), and the Health Insurance Portability and Accountability Act (HIPAA) in the United States are examples of regulatory frameworks that mandate data protection and privacy practices. Compliance with these regulations is not only a legal obligation but also a vital component of maintaining customer trust and protecting digital assets.

Organizations must develop and implement comprehensive cybersecurity policies that outline best practices, roles, and responsibilities. These policies should cover areas such as data protection, access control, incident response, and employee training. Regular audits and assessments help ensure that policies are being followed and identify areas for improvement. Incident response plans are particularly important, providing a structured approach for addressing and mitigating the impact of cyberattacks. These plans should include clear procedures for detecting, reporting, and responding to incidents, as well as mechanisms for communication and coordination.

Human factors are a critical, yet often overlooked, aspect of cybersecurity. Cybersecurity is not solely the responsibility of IT departments; it requires the active participation and vigilance of all employees. Human error, negligence, or malicious behavior can undermine even the most advanced technological defenses. Training and awareness programs are essential for educating employees about cybersecurity risks and best practices. These programs should cover topics such as password security, recognizing phishing attempts, and safe browsing habits. Encouraging a culture of security mindfulness empowers employees to act as the first line of defense against cyber threats.

Insider threats, whether intentional or unintentional, pose significant risks to organizations. Employees with access to sensitive information can inadvertently or maliciously compromise data security. Implementing strict access controls and regularly reviewing permissions help mitigate the risk of insider threats. Monitoring employee activity and using behavior analytics can identify suspicious behavior, enabling proactive measures to prevent security breaches.

The rise of cloud computing has introduced new cybersecurity challenges and opportunities. Cloud services offer scalability, flexibility, and cost savings, but they also require robust security measures to protect data and applications. Shared responsibility models delineate the security responsibilities of cloud service providers and their customers. Organizations must ensure that their cloud providers adhere to stringent security standards and implement their own measures to secure data stored in the cloud. This includes encrypting data, using MFA, and regularly monitoring cloud environments for vulnerabilities and threats.

The Internet of Things (IoT) presents another frontier for cybersecurity. IoT devices, ranging from smart home appliances to industrial sensors, generate vast amounts of data and offer numerous benefits. However, their proliferation also increases the attack surface, as many IoT devices have limited security features and can be easily compromised. Securing IoT devices requires a combination of strong authentication, encryption, and regular firmware updates. Network segmentation can also help isolate IoT devices from critical systems, reducing the potential impact of a breach.

Cybersecurity is a dynamic and evolving field, constantly adapting to new threats and technologies. Staying ahead of cybercriminals requires continuous innovation, research, and collaboration. Cybersecurity professionals must keep abreast of the latest trends and developments, participate in threat intelligence sharing, and engage in ongoing education and training. Public-private partnerships and international cooperation are essential for addressing global cyber threats and enhancing collective security.

Artificial intelligence (AI) and machine learning (ML) are emerging as powerful tools in the cybersecurity arsenal. AI and ML can analyze vast amounts of data to identify patterns and anomalies indicative of cyber threats. These technologies can automate threat detection, response, and remediation, significantly reducing the time and effort required to manage cybersecurity incidents. However, the use of AI and ML in cybersecurity also raises concerns about the potential for adversarial attacks, where cybercriminals manipulate AI systems to evade detection or cause harm. Ensuring the robustness and reliability of AI-driven security solutions is a critical area of research and development.

Cybersecurity is not just a technical issue; it is also a strategic business imperative. The financial and reputational consequences of a cyberattack can be severe, affecting customer trust, stock prices, and overall business continuity. Executive leadership must prioritize cybersecurity and allocate the necessary resources to build and maintain a strong security posture. This includes investing in technology, training, and personnel, as well as fostering a culture of security awareness throughout the organization.

In conclusion, cybersecurity imperatives are essential for protecting digital assets in an increasingly connected and digital world. The complexity and sophistication of cyber threats demand a comprehensive and multifaceted approach that integrates technological defenses, policy frameworks, and human factors. By implementing robust security measures, complying with regulations, and fostering a culture of security awareness, organizations can safeguard their digital assets, maintain customer trust, and ensure business continuity. The evolving nature of cyber threats requires continuous vigilance, innovation, and collaboration, as cybersecurity remains a critical and dynamic field. As technology continues to advance, so too must our efforts to protect and secure the digital realm, ensuring a safe and resilient future for all.

ϼϼϼ

"Virtual and augmented reality are transforming user experiences across industries. These technologies offer immersive and interactive ways to engage with content. Let's explore their potential while ensuring they enhance, not replace, human interaction."

# TWELVE

# Smart Cities and IoT - Connecting Urban Environments

The concept of smart cities represents a transformative approach to urban development, leveraging the Internet of Things (IoT) to create more connected, efficient, and sustainable urban environments. As the global population increasingly gravitates towards urban centers, cities face the challenge of managing resources and services efficiently to enhance the quality of life for their residents. Smart cities aim to address these challenges by integrating technology and data analytics into urban planning and management, enabling cities to operate more intelligently and respond dynamically to the needs of their inhabitants.

Smart cities utilize IoT devices and sensors to collect data across various domains such as transportation, energy, water management, waste management, public safety, and environmental monitoring. These interconnected devices generate vast amounts of data that can be analyzed to gain insights and optimize city operations. For instance, smart traffic management systems use sensors and cameras to monitor traffic flow, adjust traffic signals in real-time, and reduce congestion. By analyzing traffic patterns, cities can develop more efficient public transportation routes, promote alternative modes of transportation, and reduce carbon emissions.

Energy management is a critical component of smart cities, as urban areas consume a significant portion of the world's energy. Smart grids, powered by IoT technology, enable more efficient distribution and consumption of electricity. These grids use sensors and smart meters to monitor energy usage in real-time, allowing utilities to balance supply and demand more effectively. Additionally, smart grids can integrate renewable energy sources, such as solar and wind, into the energy mix, enhancing sustainability. By providing consumers with real-time information about their energy consumption, smart grids empower individuals and businesses to make more informed decisions about their energy use, leading to cost savings and reduced environmental impact.

Water management is another area where smart city technology can have a profound impact. IoT sensors can monitor water quality, detect leaks, and manage water distribution systems to ensure efficient use of this precious resource. For example, smart irrigation systems can adjust watering schedules based on weather conditions and soil moisture levels, reducing water waste in landscaping and agriculture. In addition, real-time monitoring of water infrastructure helps cities quickly identify and address issues such as pipe bursts or contamination, ensuring a reliable and safe water supply for residents.

Waste management in smart cities is enhanced through the use of IoT-enabled bins and sensors that monitor waste levels and optimize collection routes. By collecting data on waste generation and disposal patterns, cities can develop more efficient recycling programs and reduce landfill use. Smart waste management systems can also detect hazardous materials and ensure they are handled appropriately, protecting public health and the environment. Furthermore, these systems can engage residents in waste reduction efforts by providing feedback on their recycling habits and encouraging sustainable practices.

Public safety is a paramount concern for urban areas, and smart city technology offers innovative solutions to enhance security and emergency response. IoT-enabled surveillance cameras, combined with advanced analytics, can detect suspicious activities and alert authorities in real-time. Smart street lighting systems can adjust brightness based on pedestrian activity, improving visibility and safety while conserving energy. In the event of natural disasters or emergencies, smart city infrastructure can facilitate rapid communication and coordination among emergency responders, ensuring timely and effective interventions.

Environmental monitoring is crucial for maintaining the health and well-being of urban populations. Smart cities deploy IoT sensors to monitor air quality, noise levels, and other environmental factors. This data can be used to identify pollution sources, develop mitigation strategies, and inform policy decisions. For example, cities can implement low-emission zones or promote the use of electric vehicles to reduce air pollution. By providing real-time information on environmental conditions, smart cities empower residents to make healthier choices and advocate for environmental improvements.

Transportation is a key focus area for smart city initiatives, as efficient mobility is essential for economic vitality and quality of life. IoT technology enables the development of intelligent transportation systems that optimize traffic flow, reduce congestion, and enhance public transit services. For example, smart traffic lights can adjust their timing based on real-time traffic conditions, minimizing delays and improving travel times. Connected vehicles can communicate with each other and with infrastructure to avoid collisions and reduce accidents. Public transportation systems can use data analytics to predict demand, optimize schedules, and improve service reliability.

Bicycle and pedestrian infrastructure can also benefit from smart city technology. IoT-enabled bike-sharing programs allow users to locate and rent bicycles through mobile apps, promoting sustainable transportation options. Smart crosswalks can enhance pedestrian safety by detecting when people are crossing and activating warning signals for drivers. By encouraging active transportation, smart cities can reduce traffic congestion, lower emissions, and promote healthier lifestyles.

The integration of IoT in smart cities extends to buildings and infrastructure. Smart buildings use sensors and automation systems to optimize energy use, improve indoor air quality, and enhance occupant comfort. For example, smart HVAC systems can adjust temperature settings based on occupancy patterns, reducing energy consumption and costs. Building management systems can monitor and control lighting, security, and maintenance functions, streamlining operations and improving efficiency. Smart infrastructure, such as bridges and roads, can be equipped with sensors to monitor structural integrity and detect maintenance needs, preventing costly repairs and ensuring public safety.

Citizen engagement is a critical aspect of smart city initiatives, as the success of these projects depends on the active participation and support of residents. Digital platforms and mobile apps enable cities to communicate with citizens, gather feedback, and involve them in decision-making processes. For example, cities can use apps to notify residents of public meetings, solicit input on urban planning projects, and report issues such as potholes or streetlight outages.

By fostering a sense of community and collaboration, smart cities can build trust and ensure that their initiatives reflect the needs and priorities of their inhabitants.

Smart cities also face several challenges that must be addressed to realize their full potential. One of the primary challenges is data privacy and security. The extensive use of IoT devices and data collection raises concerns about the protection of personal information and the potential for cyberattacks. Cities must implement robust cybersecurity measures to safeguard data and ensure the privacy of residents. This includes encrypting data transmissions, securing IoT devices, and establishing clear data governance policies. Additionally, transparency and accountability are essential for building public trust in smart city initiatives. Cities must be transparent about their data collection practices and provide residents with control over their personal information.

The digital divide is another challenge that smart cities must address to ensure equitable access to technology and services. Not all residents have access to high-speed internet, smartphones, or digital literacy skills, which can create disparities in the benefits of smart city initiatives. To bridge this gap, cities must invest in digital infrastructure, provide affordable internet access, and offer training programs to enhance digital literacy. By promoting inclusivity, smart cities can ensure that all residents benefit from technological advancements.

Funding and sustainability are also critical considerations for smart city projects. Implementing and maintaining smart city infrastructure requires significant financial investment, and cities must develop sustainable funding models to support these initiatives. Public-private partnerships can play a crucial role in providing financial resources and expertise. Additionally, cities must consider the long-term sustainability of their projects, ensuring that they can adapt to changing technologies and evolving needs. This involves continuous evaluation and optimization of smart city systems, as well as planning for future upgrades and expansions.

Collaboration and interoperability are essential for the success of smart city initiatives. Smart city systems often involve multiple stakeholders, including government agencies, private companies, and academic institutions. Effective collaboration requires clear communication, shared goals, and coordinated efforts. Interoperability is also critical, as smart city systems must be able to communicate and work seamlessly with each other. Developing common standards and protocols can facilitate interoperability and ensure that different systems can integrate and exchange data effectively.

The future of smart cities is promising, with advancements in technology driving continued innovation and improvement. Emerging technologies such as artificial intelligence, 5G, and blockchain have the potential to enhance smart city capabilities and address existing challenges. AI can provide more advanced data analytics and predictive insights, enabling cities to make more informed decisions and respond proactively to issues. 5G technology will offer faster and more reliable connectivity, supporting the proliferation of IoT devices and real-time data processing. Blockchain can enhance data security and transparency, ensuring the integrity and trustworthiness of smart city systems.

The integration of smart city technologies can transform urban environments, making them more efficient, sustainable, and responsive to the needs of residents. By harnessing the power of IoT and data analytics, cities can optimize resource management, improve public services, and enhance the quality of life for their inhabitants. However, realizing the full potential of smart cities requires addressing challenges related to data privacy, digital inclusion, funding, collaboration, and sustainability. Through thoughtful planning, innovative solutions, and active engagement with residents, smart cities can create a more connected and resilient future for urban environments worldwide.

ÞÞÞ

"Social media marketing is a powerful way to build brand awareness and loyalty. Authentic engagement and quality content are key to success. Harness the power of social media to create lasting connections with your audience."

# THIRTEEN

# The Sharing Economy – Collaborative Consumption Trends

The sharing economy has emerged as a transformative force in the modern economic landscape, fundamentally altering how goods and services are accessed and consumed. Rooted in principles of collaboration and resource optimization, the sharing economy encompasses various models of collaborative consumption, where individuals share access to products and services rather than owning them outright. This paradigm shift is driven by advancements in digital technology, changing consumer behaviors, and the desire for more sustainable and efficient use of resources. By facilitating peer-to-peer exchanges and leveraging underutilized assets, the sharing economy has created new opportunities for individuals and businesses while challenging traditional notions of ownership and consumption.

At the core of the sharing economy is the concept of maximizing the utility of resources through sharing. This approach contrasts sharply with the traditional linear consumption model, where goods are produced, purchased, used, and then discarded. Instead, the sharing economy promotes a circular model where products and services are continuously utilized by multiple users, reducing waste and promoting sustainability. Digital platforms and mobile apps play a crucial role in enabling these exchanges, providing the infrastructure for individuals to connect, share, and transact with ease.

One of the most prominent examples of the sharing economy is the rise of ride-sharing services such as Uber and Lyft. These platforms connect drivers with passengers seeking transportation, offering a flexible and cost-effective alternative to traditional taxi services. By utilizing personal vehicles and leveraging real-time data, ride-sharing services optimize transportation resources and reduce the need for car ownership. This model benefits both drivers, who can earn income by offering rides, and passengers, who enjoy convenient and affordable transportation options. The success of ride-sharing has sparked the growth of other mobility services, including bike-sharing and scooter-sharing, further expanding the reach of the sharing economy in urban transportation.

Accommodation sharing is another significant component of the sharing economy, with platforms like Airbnb leading the way. Airbnb allows homeowners to rent out their properties or spare rooms to travelers, providing a diverse range of lodging options that often offer more personalized and unique experiences than traditional hotels. This model benefits property owners by generating additional income from underutilized spaces and benefits travelers by offering more affordable and varied accommodation choices. The popularity of accommodation sharing has also stimulated local economies by increasing tourism and supporting small businesses.

The sharing economy extends beyond transportation and accommodation to include a wide range of goods and services. For example, platforms like Rent the Runway enable users to rent high-end fashion items for special occasions, reducing the need for purchasing expensive clothing that may only be worn once. Similarly, tool-sharing services allow individuals to borrow tools and equipment for home improvement projects, avoiding the cost and storage issues associated with owning seldom-used items. These models of collaborative consumption promote efficient resource use and provide consumers with access to goods and services that might otherwise be financially out of reach.

Another area where the sharing economy has made significant inroads is in the realm of coworking spaces. Coworking spaces offer flexible, shared office environments where individuals and businesses can rent desks or offices on a short-term basis. This model caters to freelancers, startups, and remote workers who seek a professional workspace without the long-term commitment and expense of traditional office leases. Coworking spaces foster collaboration and networking, creating vibrant communities of professionals from diverse fields. By optimizing the use of office space and resources, coworking spaces contribute to a more efficient and dynamic work environment.

The rise of the sharing economy has also been fueled by changing consumer attitudes and behaviors. Millennials and younger generations, in particular, prioritize access over ownership, valuing experiences and convenience over the accumulation of material possessions. This shift is influenced by several factors, including economic constraints, environmental concerns, and the desire for greater flexibility and mobility. The sharing economy aligns with these values by offering cost-effective, sustainable, and flexible alternatives to traditional consumption models.

Sustainability is a key driver of the sharing economy, as collaborative consumption inherently promotes the efficient use of resources and reduces waste. By sharing goods and services, individuals can decrease their environmental footprint and contribute to a more sustainable economy. For example, ride-sharing reduces the number of vehicles on the road, lowering greenhouse gas emissions and easing traffic congestion. Similarly, accommodation sharing maximizes the use of existing housing infrastructure, reducing the need for new construction and the associated environmental impact. The sharing economy also encourages the reuse and recycling of products, extending their lifespan and reducing the demand for new manufacturing.

The economic benefits of the sharing economy are significant, providing new income opportunities for individuals and fostering entrepreneurship. By leveraging underutilized assets, individuals can monetize their resources and generate additional income. This is particularly valuable in times of economic uncertainty or for those seeking flexible work arrangements. The sharing economy also lowers barriers to entry for new businesses, enabling entrepreneurs to launch ventures with minimal upfront investment. Digital platforms facilitate access to a global market, allowing small businesses and freelancers to reach a wider audience and grow their enterprises.

Despite its many advantages, the sharing economy also presents several challenges and controversies. One of the primary concerns is the regulatory environment, as traditional industries and regulators struggle to adapt to the rapidly evolving landscape of collaborative consumption. Ride-sharing and accommodation-sharing platforms, for example, have faced legal and regulatory hurdles related to licensing, safety standards, and taxation. Balancing innovation with consumer protection and fair competition is a complex task that requires ongoing dialogue and collaboration between stakeholders.

Another significant challenge is the issue of labor rights and working conditions in the sharing economy. Many workers in the sharing economy operate as independent contractors, lacking the benefits and protections afforded to traditional employees. This has raised concerns about job security, fair wages, and access to benefits such as health insurance and retirement plans. Addressing these issues requires a reevaluation of labor laws and the development of new policies that protect workers while preserving the flexibility that is central to the sharing economy.

Data privacy and security are also critical concerns in the sharing economy. Digital platforms collect vast amounts of personal data to facilitate transactions and improve services. Ensuring the security of this data and protecting user privacy is paramount, as data breaches and misuse can erode trust and undermine the viability of sharing economy platforms. Companies must implement robust data protection measures and comply with regulations to safeguard user information and maintain consumer confidence.

The sharing economy has the potential to exacerbate existing inequalities if not managed thoughtfully. While collaborative consumption can provide economic opportunities, it may also concentrate benefits among those with access to digital platforms and valuable assets. Ensuring equitable access to the sharing economy and addressing disparities in participation are essential for realizing its full potential. This includes expanding digital literacy and connectivity, as well as developing inclusive policies that promote diverse participation.

Looking ahead, the sharing economy is poised for continued growth and innovation. Emerging technologies such as blockchain, artificial intelligence, and the Internet of Things (IoT) are likely to enhance and expand collaborative consumption models.

Blockchain technology, for example, can increase transparency and trust in peer-to-peer transactions by providing a secure, decentralized ledger for recording exchanges. AI can improve matchmaking and personalization, enhancing user experiences and optimizing resource utilization. IoT devices can facilitate real-time monitoring and management of shared resources, increasing efficiency and convenience.

The sharing economy also has the potential to drive social change by fostering a sense of community and collaboration. By encouraging individuals to share and connect, collaborative consumption can strengthen social ties and promote a culture of cooperation and mutual support. This is particularly valuable in urban environments, where the anonymity and isolation of city living can be mitigated through shared experiences and collective engagement.

In conclusion, the sharing economy represents a significant shift in how goods and services are accessed and consumed, driven by digital technology, changing consumer behaviors, and a focus on sustainability. By enabling collaborative consumption, the sharing economy optimizes resource use, reduces waste, and provides economic opportunities for individuals and businesses. However, realizing the full potential of the sharing economy requires addressing challenges related to regulation, labor rights, data privacy, and equity. As the sharing economy continues to evolve, it holds the promise of creating more connected, efficient, and resilient communities. By embracing the principles of collaboration and resource optimization, the sharing economy can contribute to a more sustainable and inclusive future.

"Corporate social responsibility is the cornerstone of modern business. Companies that prioritize ethical practices and social impact build stronger brands. CSR is not just good for society; it's good for business."

# FOURTEEN

## HEALTH TECH ADVANCES – IMPROVING HEALTHCARE DELIVERY

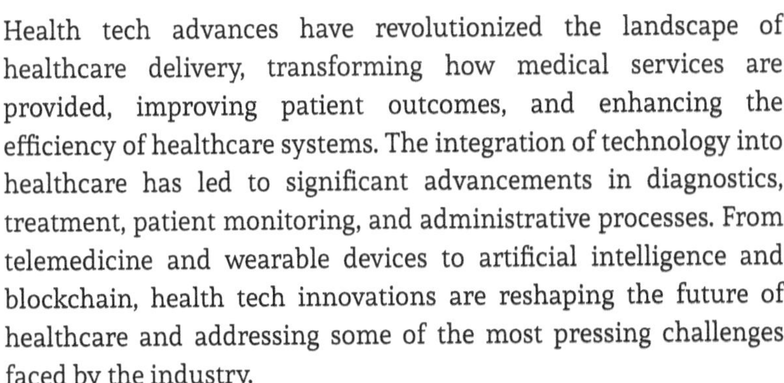

Health tech advances have revolutionized the landscape of healthcare delivery, transforming how medical services are provided, improving patient outcomes, and enhancing the efficiency of healthcare systems. The integration of technology into healthcare has led to significant advancements in diagnostics, treatment, patient monitoring, and administrative processes. From telemedicine and wearable devices to artificial intelligence and blockchain, health tech innovations are reshaping the future of healthcare and addressing some of the most pressing challenges faced by the industry.

One of the most impactful advancements in health tech is the rise of telemedicine. Telemedicine leverages digital communication technologies to provide remote clinical services, enabling patients to consult with healthcare providers from the comfort of their homes. This approach has proven especially valuable in rural and underserved areas, where access to healthcare facilities may be limited. By eliminating geographical barriers, telemedicine expands access to care, reduces travel time and costs, and increases convenience for patients. It also allows healthcare providers to reach a larger patient population and manage chronic conditions more effectively through regular virtual check-ins.

Telemedicine gained widespread adoption during the COVID-19 pandemic, as social distancing measures and lockdowns necessitated remote consultations. The pandemic highlighted the potential of telemedicine to maintain continuity of care while minimizing the risk of infection. Moving forward, telemedicine is expected to remain a key component of healthcare delivery, supported by advancements in video conferencing, secure data transmission, and digital health records. The integration of telemedicine with other health tech innovations, such as wearable devices and remote monitoring, further enhances its effectiveness and reach.

Wearable devices have become an integral part of modern healthcare, providing continuous monitoring of various health parameters. These devices, which include smartwatches, fitness trackers, and medical-grade wearables, can monitor heart rate, blood pressure, glucose levels, and physical activity. By collecting real-time data, wearables enable early detection of health issues, prompt intervention, and personalized treatment plans. For example, a wearable device that monitors cardiac activity can alert users and healthcare providers to irregularities, allowing for timely diagnosis and management of potential heart conditions.

The data collected by wearable devices can also empower patients to take a more active role in managing their health. By providing insights into their daily habits and health metrics, wearables encourage individuals to make informed lifestyle choices, such as increasing physical activity or adhering to medication regimens. Additionally, healthcare providers can use this data to track patient progress, adjust treatment plans, and provide more personalized care. The integration of wearable technology with electronic health records (EHRs) ensures that healthcare providers have access to comprehensive and up-to-date patient information, facilitating better clinical decision-making.

Artificial intelligence (AI) and machine learning (ML) are transforming healthcare delivery by enabling advanced data analysis, predictive analytics, and decision support systems. AI algorithms can process vast amounts of medical data to identify patterns, predict outcomes, and recommend treatments. In diagnostics, AI-powered tools can analyze medical images, such as X-rays, MRIs, and CT scans, with remarkable accuracy, assisting radiologists in detecting abnormalities and diagnosing conditions. For example, AI algorithms have been developed to identify early signs of diseases such as cancer, diabetic retinopathy, and Alzheimer's, improving the chances of early intervention and successful treatment.

Predictive analytics, powered by AI and ML, can anticipate patient needs and identify individuals at risk of developing specific conditions. By analyzing historical health data, demographic information, and lifestyle factors, predictive models can forecast the likelihood of hospital readmissions, disease progression, and adverse events. This proactive approach allows healthcare providers to implement preventive measures, allocate resources more efficiently, and improve patient outcomes. For instance, predictive analytics can help identify patients at risk of chronic diseases, enabling targeted interventions and personalized care plans.

AI and ML also play a crucial role in drug discovery and

development. The traditional process of developing new drugs is time-consuming and costly, often taking years of research and billions of dollars. AI algorithms can analyze large datasets of biological and chemical information to identify potential drug candidates, predict their efficacy, and optimize clinical trial designs. This accelerates the drug discovery process, reduces costs, and increases the likelihood of finding effective treatments. Furthermore, AI can identify existing drugs that may be repurposed for new therapeutic uses, providing faster and more cost-effective solutions to emerging health challenges.

Blockchain technology is another health tech innovation that holds promise for improving healthcare delivery. Blockchain provides a secure, decentralized, and immutable ledger for recording transactions and sharing data. In healthcare, blockchain can enhance the security and interoperability of electronic health records, ensuring that patient data is accurate, accessible, and protected from unauthorized access. By enabling secure data sharing between healthcare providers, patients, and researchers, blockchain fosters collaboration and improves the continuity of care.

One of the key benefits of blockchain in healthcare is its potential to address data privacy and security concerns. Patient data breaches and cyberattacks are significant issues in the healthcare industry, compromising sensitive information and undermining trust. Blockchain's encryption and decentralized architecture make it more resilient to hacking attempts, ensuring that patient data remains confidential and secure. Additionally, blockchain can provide patients with greater control over their health data, allowing them to grant or revoke access to specific information as needed.

Blockchain can also streamline administrative processes and reduce inefficiencies in healthcare systems. For example, blockchain can automate the verification of credentials for healthcare professionals, ensuring that they meet the necessary qualifications and certifications. This reduces administrative burdens and accelerates the hiring and onboarding process. In supply chain management, blockchain can track the provenance and authenticity of pharmaceuticals, preventing counterfeit drugs from entering the market and ensuring the integrity of the supply chain.

The integration of health tech innovations into healthcare delivery requires careful consideration of ethical, regulatory, and practical challenges. Ensuring the privacy and security of patient data is paramount, as the increased use of digital technologies introduces new vulnerabilities. Healthcare providers and technology companies must adhere to strict data protection regulations, such as the Health Insurance Portability and Accountability Act (HIPAA) in the United States and the General Data Protection Regulation (GDPR) in the European Union. Implementing robust cybersecurity measures, such as encryption, access controls, and regular security audits, is essential for safeguarding patient information.

Ethical considerations also arise in the use of AI and machine learning in healthcare. Bias in AI algorithms can lead to disparities in diagnosis and treatment, disproportionately affecting certain populations. Ensuring the fairness and transparency of AI systems requires diverse and representative training data, continuous monitoring for bias, and collaboration with ethicists and stakeholders. Additionally, the use of AI in clinical decision-making should complement, not replace, the expertise of healthcare professionals. Maintaining human oversight and accountability is crucial for ensuring that AI-driven recommendations are accurate and appropriate.

The successful implementation of health tech innovations also depends on the integration and interoperability of different systems. Healthcare providers often use a variety of electronic health record systems, medical devices, and software applications, which can create data silos and hinder information sharing. Interoperability standards and frameworks, such as Fast Healthcare Interoperability Resources (FHIR), facilitate the seamless exchange of health data across different systems and platforms. Achieving interoperability requires collaboration between technology vendors, healthcare providers, and regulatory bodies to establish common standards and protocols.

Training and education are essential for healthcare professionals to effectively utilize health tech innovations. As technology becomes more integrated into clinical practice, healthcare providers must develop the skills and knowledge to leverage these tools for patient care. This includes understanding the capabilities and limitations of AI algorithms, interpreting data from wearable devices, and using telemedicine platforms for remote consultations. Continuous professional development and training programs can ensure that healthcare providers stay current with technological advancements and best practices.

Health tech advances are also transforming the patient experience, empowering individuals to take an active role in managing their health. Patient portals and mobile health apps provide convenient access to health information, appointment scheduling, medication reminders, and secure communication with healthcare providers. These tools enhance patient engagement and adherence to treatment plans, leading to better health outcomes. For example, a diabetes management app can track blood glucose levels, provide dietary recommendations, and connect patients with support groups, helping them manage their condition more effectively.

The future of healthcare delivery will be shaped by the continued integration of health tech innovations. Emerging technologies, such as genomics, nanotechnology, and 3D printing, hold the potential to further revolutionize healthcare. Genomics can provide insights into an individual's genetic makeup, enabling personalized medicine and targeted therapies. Nanotechnology offers new possibilities for drug delivery and disease detection at the molecular level. 3D printing can create customized medical devices, prosthetics, and even human tissue, improving the precision and effectiveness of treatments.

Telemedicine and remote monitoring are expected to play a central role in the future of healthcare, driven by advancements in communication technologies and increasing patient acceptance. The expansion of telehealth services will improve access to care, particularly for populations in remote or underserved areas. Remote monitoring, supported by wearable devices and IoT sensors, will enable continuous health assessment and early detection of potential issues, allowing for timely interventions and reducing hospital admissions.

The integration of artificial intelligence into healthcare will continue to evolve, with AI becoming more sophisticated and capable of supporting a broader range of clinical tasks. AI-powered decision support systems will assist healthcare providers in diagnosing complex conditions, predicting patient outcomes, and developing personalized treatment plans. The collaboration between human expertise and AI will enhance the accuracy and efficiency of healthcare delivery, ultimately improving patient care.

In conclusion, health tech advances are transforming healthcare delivery by improving access, efficiency, and patient outcomes. Telemedicine, wearable devices, artificial intelligence, and blockchain are just a few of the innovations reshaping the healthcare landscape. While these technologies offer significant benefits, their successful implementation requires addressing challenges related to data privacy, ethical considerations, interoperability, and education. As technology continues to advance, the future of healthcare holds immense promise, with new innovations driving progress and improving the quality of care for patients worldwide. By embracing health tech advances and fostering collaboration between stakeholders, healthcare systems can achieve greater efficiency, sustainability, and patient satisfaction.

ppp

*"The ethics of innovation requires balancing progress with responsibility. Every new technology brings both opportunities and challenges. Ethical innovation ensures that advancements benefit humanity as a whole."*

# FIFTEEN

# EdTech and Online Learning - Transforming Education

The transformation of education through EdTech and online learning is a profound and ongoing process that has fundamentally altered the landscape of teaching and learning. Educational technology, or EdTech, encompasses a wide range of digital tools and platforms designed to enhance the educational experience for students, educators, and institutions.

Online learning, as a component of EdTech, provides flexibility and accessibility, breaking down traditional barriers to education and creating opportunities for lifelong learning. Together, these advancements are reshaping how education is delivered, accessed, and experienced.

One of the most significant impacts of EdTech is the democratization of education. Traditional education systems have often been limited by geography, resources, and infrastructure, making it difficult for many individuals to access quality education. EdTech and online learning platforms have the potential to bridge these gaps by providing access to a wealth of educational resources from anywhere in the world.

Platforms like Coursera, edX, and Khan Academy offer courses from top universities and institutions, allowing learners to access high-quality education regardless of their location. This accessibility is particularly beneficial for individuals in remote or underserved areas who may not have access to traditional educational institutions.

The flexibility offered by online learning is another transformative aspect. Unlike traditional classroom settings that require fixed schedules and physical attendance, online learning allows students to learn at their own pace and on their own time.

This flexibility is especially valuable for working professionals, parents, and others with demanding schedules who wish to continue their education. Online courses and programs can be tailored to fit around existing commitments, enabling learners to balance education with work, family, and other responsibilities.

EdTech also enhances the personalization of education, catering to the unique needs and learning styles of individual students. Adaptive learning technologies use data and analytics to assess a student's progress and adjust the content and pace of instruction accordingly.

This personalized approach ensures that students receive the support they need to master the material, leading to improved learning outcomes. For example, platforms like DreamBox and Knewton use adaptive learning algorithms to provide personalized math and science instruction, helping students build a strong foundation in these critical subjects.

The integration of multimedia and interactive elements in EdTech platforms enriches the learning experience and caters to different learning preferences. Videos, simulations, games, and interactive quizzes make learning more engaging and enjoyable. For instance, platforms like Duolingo use gamification to teach languages, incorporating elements of competition and reward to motivate learners. Interactive simulations in subjects like physics and chemistry allow students to experiment and explore concepts in a virtual environment, making abstract ideas more concrete and understandable.

Collaboration and communication are essential components of effective learning, and EdTech facilitates these interactions in new and innovative ways. Online discussion forums, group projects, and virtual classrooms enable students to collaborate with peers and instructors regardless of their physical location. Tools like Zoom, Microsoft Teams, and Google Classroom provide real-time communication and collaboration features, creating a sense of community and connection among online learners.

These platforms support synchronous learning, where students and instructors interact in real-time, as well as asynchronous learning, where interactions occur at different times to accommodate diverse schedules.

Assessment and feedback are critical aspects of the learning process, and EdTech offers new ways to evaluate student performance and provide timely feedback. Online assessments can include quizzes, assignments, and exams that are automatically graded, providing instant feedback to students. This immediate feedback helps students identify areas where they need improvement and reinforces their understanding of the material.

Advanced analytics and machine learning can also be used to

analyze student performance data, providing insights into learning patterns and helping educators tailor their instruction to better meet student needs.

The role of teachers and educators is evolving with the integration of EdTech and online learning. Rather than being the sole source of knowledge, teachers are becoming facilitators and guides who support students in their learning journey. EdTech tools enable teachers to create more dynamic and interactive lessons, incorporating a variety of multimedia resources to enhance instruction.

Teachers can also use data and analytics to monitor student progress and intervene when necessary, providing targeted support and guidance. Professional development and training in EdTech are essential for educators to effectively leverage these tools and maximize their impact on student learning.

The COVID-19 pandemic has accelerated the adoption of EdTech and online learning, highlighting their importance in ensuring the continuity of education during disruptions. As schools and universities around the world closed their doors to prevent the spread of the virus, educators and students quickly transitioned to online learning platforms.

This rapid shift underscored the potential of EdTech to provide flexible and resilient educational solutions. While the pandemic presented significant challenges, it also demonstrated the feasibility and benefits of integrating technology into education on a large scale.

Despite the many advantages of EdTech and online learning, there are also challenges and considerations that must be addressed to ensure their effective implementation. Digital equity is a critical issue, as not all students have access to the necessary technology and internet connectivity to participate in online learning.

Bridging the digital divide requires investment in infrastructure, devices, and support for students and families to ensure that all learners can benefit from EdTech. Additionally, educators must be trained and supported in using EdTech tools effectively, as the successful integration of technology into education depends on the skills and confidence of teachers.

Student engagement is another challenge in online learning environments. Without the physical presence of a classroom and face-to-face interactions with peers and instructors, some students may struggle to stay motivated and focused. To address this, EdTech platforms must prioritize engaging and interactive content that captures students' interest and encourages active participation.

Strategies such as gamification, interactive simulations, and project-based learning can help maintain student engagement and foster a sense of connection and community.

Data privacy and security are also critical considerations in the implementation of EdTech. As students and educators increasingly rely on digital platforms, protecting sensitive information and ensuring compliance with data protection regulations is paramount. EdTech providers and educational institutions must implement robust security measures to safeguard student data and maintain trust. Clear policies and practices regarding data collection, storage, and use are essential to protect the privacy of students and educators.

Looking ahead, the future of EdTech and online learning is poised for continued innovation and growth. Emerging technologies such as artificial intelligence, virtual reality, and augmented reality hold the potential to further transform education. AI can enhance personalized learning by providing more accurate and timely insights into student performance and tailoring instruction to individual needs.

Virtual reality and augmented reality can create immersive and interactive learning experiences, allowing students to explore complex concepts in a virtual environment. For example, VR can be used to conduct virtual field trips, enabling students to visit historical sites or explore scientific phenomena without leaving the classroom.

The integration of blockchain technology into EdTech offers new possibilities for credentialing and verifying academic achievements. Blockchain can provide a secure and transparent way to record and verify educational credentials, making it easier for students to share their achievements with employers and institutions. This technology can also streamline administrative processes, reducing the burden of record-keeping and ensuring the integrity of academic records.

Collaboration between educational institutions, technology providers, and policymakers is essential to realize the full potential of EdTech and online learning. Developing a supportive ecosystem that fosters innovation, addresses challenges, and promotes best practices is crucial for the successful integration of technology into education.

Public-private partnerships can facilitate investment in infrastructure, research, and development, ensuring that EdTech solutions are accessible and effective for all learners.

The global nature of EdTech and online learning also presents opportunities for cross-cultural exchange and collaboration. Online platforms can connect students and educators from different parts of the world, fostering cultural understanding and broadening perspectives.

Collaborative projects and virtual exchanges can enrich the learning experience and prepare students for a globalized world. Additionally, sharing best practices and lessons learned from different educational contexts can drive innovation and improve the effectiveness of EdTech solutions.

In conclusion, EdTech and online learning are transforming education by providing greater accessibility, flexibility, and personalization. These advancements are democratizing education, enabling lifelong learning, and preparing students for the demands of the digital age.

While challenges such as digital equity, student engagement, and data privacy must be addressed, the potential benefits of EdTech are immense. Continued innovation and collaboration among stakeholders will be key to harnessing the full potential of technology in education and creating a more inclusive, effective, and resilient educational landscape. As we move forward, the integration of EdTech and online learning will continue to shape the future of education, empowering learners and educators and enhancing the quality of education worldwide.

ᐅᐅᐅ

*"The future of retail lies in blending online and offline experiences. Omnichannel strategies create a seamless customer journey. By integrating digital and physical touchpoints, retailers can meet the evolving needs of consumers."*

# SIXTEEN

## VIRTUAL AND AUGMENTED REALITY - ENHANCING USER EXPERIENCES

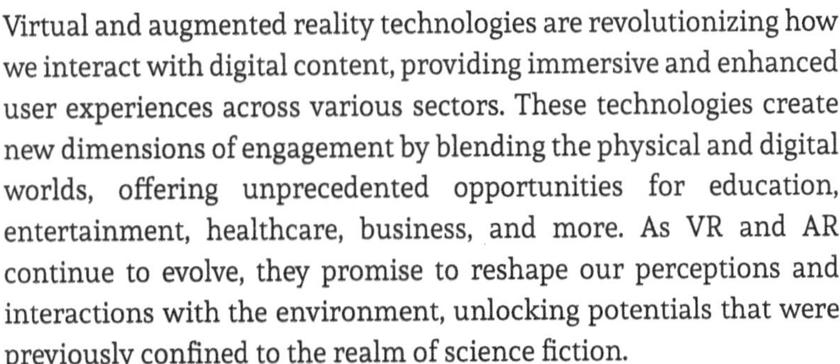

Virtual and augmented reality technologies are revolutionizing how we interact with digital content, providing immersive and enhanced user experiences across various sectors. These technologies create new dimensions of engagement by blending the physical and digital worlds, offering unprecedented opportunities for education, entertainment, healthcare, business, and more. As VR and AR continue to evolve, they promise to reshape our perceptions and interactions with the environment, unlocking potentials that were previously confined to the realm of science fiction.

Virtual reality (VR) immerses users in a fully digital environment, cutting off their senses from the physical world and transporting them to a computer-generated space. This is typically achieved through headsets equipped with screens, sensors, and audio devices that respond to the user's movements, creating a sense of presence in the virtual world. The development of VR technology has made significant strides, with devices such as the Oculus Rift, HTC Vive, and PlayStation VR providing high-quality immersive experiences. These advancements have made VR more accessible to consumers, driving its adoption in various fields.

One of the most significant impacts of VR is in the realm of entertainment and gaming. VR gaming offers players a level of immersion and interactivity that traditional gaming cannot match. By physically moving within a virtual space, players can experience games in a more engaging and realistic manner. For instance, VR can simulate the sensation of flying, diving underwater, or exploring fantastical worlds, providing an unparalleled sense of adventure and excitement. Beyond gaming, VR is being used in the film industry to create immersive storytelling experiences. Virtual reality films and 360-degree videos allow viewers to explore scenes from multiple perspectives, making them active participants in the narrative.

The educational sector is another area where VR is making a profound impact. Traditional education methods often rely on passive learning, where students absorb information through lectures and textbooks. VR transforms this approach by enabling active learning, where students can interact with educational content in a meaningful way. For example, VR can take students on virtual field trips to historical sites, natural wonders, or even the human body, providing an experiential learning experience that enhances understanding and retention. Medical students can use VR simulations to practice surgical procedures in a risk-free environment, gaining valuable hands-on experience. Similarly, engineering students can explore complex structures and systems in 3D, improving their spatial awareness and problem-solving skills.

Augmented reality (AR), on the other hand, overlays digital content onto the physical world, enhancing the user's perception of their environment. Unlike VR, which creates a separate digital space, AR integrates digital elements into the real world, allowing users to interact with both simultaneously. This is typically achieved through devices such as smartphones, tablets, and AR glasses that use cameras and sensors to detect the physical environment and overlay digital information. AR technology has seen widespread adoption through applications like Pokémon Go, which became a global phenomenon by allowing users to find and capture virtual creatures in real-world locations.

AR is also transforming various industries by providing practical and innovative solutions. In retail, AR enhances the shopping experience by allowing customers to visualize products in their environment before making a purchase. For example, furniture retailers like IKEA offer AR apps that enable users to place virtual furniture in their homes to see how it fits and looks. This not only helps customers make more informed decisions but also reduces the likelihood of returns. In the fashion industry, AR mirrors allow customers to virtually try on clothes and accessories, offering a convenient and interactive shopping experience.

In the healthcare sector, AR is being used to improve diagnostics, treatment, and patient care. AR applications can overlay medical images, such as X-rays and MRIs, onto a patient's body, providing doctors with a more accurate and intuitive understanding of internal structures. This can assist in planning surgical procedures, guiding interventions, and improving the precision of treatments. AR can also be used in rehabilitation, where patients can engage in interactive exercises that enhance their recovery process. For instance, stroke patients can use AR to perform motor skills exercises, receiving real-time feedback and motivation.

The business and enterprise sectors are leveraging AR and VR to enhance productivity and collaboration. Virtual reality is being used for training and simulation, providing employees with realistic and immersive experiences that improve skill acquisition and retention. For example, VR training modules can simulate hazardous work environments, allowing workers to practice safety protocols without the risk of injury. In corporate settings, VR can facilitate virtual meetings and conferences, enabling remote teams to collaborate in a shared virtual space. This can reduce travel costs and improve communication, particularly in the context of global organizations.

Augmented reality is also being used to enhance field service and maintenance. AR applications can provide technicians with real-time information and guidance, overlaying instructions and diagrams onto physical equipment. This can improve the efficiency and accuracy of repairs, reducing downtime and costs. Additionally, AR can be used for remote assistance, where experts can guide technicians through complex procedures using AR overlays and annotations. This enables organizations to provide high-quality support without the need for on-site visits, improving service delivery and customer satisfaction.

The integration of AR and VR in the real estate industry is transforming how properties are marketed and sold. Virtual reality tours allow potential buyers to explore properties remotely, providing a realistic sense of space and layout. This is particularly beneficial for international buyers or those unable to visit properties in person. Augmented reality can enhance physical property visits by overlaying information, such as room dimensions, material specifications, and renovation possibilities. This interactive experience helps buyers make more informed decisions and envision the potential of the property.

Despite the significant advancements and applications of AR and VR, there are challenges and considerations that must be addressed to realize their full potential. One of the primary challenges is the cost and accessibility of high-quality VR and AR devices. While prices have decreased over time, high-end VR headsets and AR glasses remain expensive, limiting their adoption among consumers and businesses. Developing more affordable and user-friendly devices is essential for widespread adoption.

Another challenge is the potential for sensory overload and motion sickness in VR environments. The immersive nature of VR can cause disorientation and discomfort for some users, particularly during prolonged use. Improving the comfort and usability of VR headsets, as well as optimizing content to minimize motion sickness, is crucial for enhancing the user experience. Similarly, AR applications must be designed to provide relevant and non-intrusive information, avoiding clutter and distraction.

Data privacy and security are critical considerations in the development and deployment of AR and VR technologies. These technologies often collect and process vast amounts of data, including location, personal preferences, and biometric information. Ensuring the privacy and security of this data is paramount, as breaches can have serious implications for users. Developers and companies must implement robust data protection measures and comply with regulations to safeguard user information and build trust.

Ethical considerations also arise in the use of AR and VR. The immersive and persuasive nature of these technologies raises questions about their potential impact on behavior and perception. For instance, the use of VR in advertising and marketing must be approached with caution to avoid manipulative or deceptive practices. Additionally, the development of realistic virtual environments and avatars raises concerns about identity and authenticity. Establishing ethical guidelines and standards for the use of AR and VR is essential to ensure their responsible and beneficial application.

Looking ahead, the future of AR and VR holds immense promise, with ongoing advancements in technology driving new possibilities. The development of more powerful and compact hardware, coupled with improvements in software and content creation, will enhance the capabilities and accessibility of AR and VR. Emerging technologies such as 5G and artificial intelligence will further enhance the performance and functionality of AR and VR applications, enabling real-time data processing and more sophisticated interactions.

One of the most exciting prospects is the convergence of AR and VR, creating mixed reality (MR) environments that seamlessly blend digital and physical worlds. Mixed reality combines the immersive qualities of VR with the interactive and contextual capabilities of AR, offering a unified and enhanced user experience. MR has the potential to transform various sectors, from education and training to entertainment and communication, providing new ways to interact with and understand the world.

In conclusion, virtual and augmented reality are transformative technologies that are enhancing user experiences across a wide range of sectors. By creating immersive and interactive environments, AR and VR offer new dimensions of engagement and understanding. While challenges such as cost, accessibility, and data privacy must be addressed, the potential benefits of AR and VR are immense. Continued innovation and development will drive the evolution of these technologies, opening up new possibilities and reshaping our interactions with the digital and physical worlds. As AR and VR become more integrated into our daily lives, they will continue to revolutionize how we learn, work, play, and connect, creating a more immersive and interconnected future.

ppp

"EdTech is revolutionizing education, making learning more accessible and personalized. Digital tools can empower students and educators alike. The future of education is bright with technology-driven innovation."

# SEVENTEEN

# THE FUTURE OF RETAIL - BLENDING ONLINE AND OFFLINE WORLDS

The future of retail is marked by a dynamic blending of online and offline worlds, creating a seamless and integrated shopping experience for consumers. As technology continues to evolve, the boundaries between digital and physical retail spaces are becoming increasingly blurred, driving innovation and transforming how businesses operate and engage with customers. This convergence is driven by changing consumer behaviors, advancements in technology, and the need for retailers to adapt to a rapidly shifting marketplace. By harnessing the power of both online and offline channels, retailers can offer personalized, convenient, and immersive shopping experiences that meet the diverse needs and preferences of modern consumers.

One of the most significant trends shaping the future of retail is the rise of omnichannel strategies. Omnichannel retailing involves creating a unified and cohesive customer experience across multiple channels, including brick-and-mortar stores, e-commerce websites, mobile apps, social media, and more. This approach recognizes that consumers no longer shop exclusively through one channel but rather move fluidly between them. For example, a customer might research a product online, visit a physical store to see it in person, and then make the purchase through a mobile app. By providing a consistent and integrated experience across all touchpoints, retailers can enhance customer satisfaction and loyalty.

A key component of omnichannel retailing is the use of data and analytics to understand customer behavior and preferences. By collecting and analyzing data from various sources, retailers can gain insights into how customers interact with different channels and tailor their strategies accordingly. For instance, data analytics can reveal patterns in online browsing and purchasing behavior, helping retailers optimize their website design and product recommendations. Similarly, data from in-store transactions can inform inventory management and merchandising decisions. By leveraging data to create a holistic view of the customer journey, retailers can deliver more personalized and relevant experiences.

Technology plays a crucial role in bridging the gap between online and offline retail worlds. One of the most impactful technologies is augmented reality (AR), which enhances the physical shopping experience by overlaying digital information onto the real world. AR applications allow customers to visualize products in their own environment before making a purchase. For example, furniture retailers like IKEA and Wayfair offer AR apps that enable customers to see how a piece of furniture would look in their home. Similarly, beauty brands like Sephora use AR to provide virtual makeup try-ons, allowing customers to experiment with different products and looks. By integrating digital content into the physical shopping experience, AR enhances engagement and reduces uncertainty, leading to higher conversion rates.

Another technology transforming retail is artificial intelligence (AI). AI-driven tools and algorithms enable retailers to offer personalized recommendations, optimize pricing strategies, and enhance customer service. For instance, AI-powered chatbots can provide instant support and answer customer inquiries, improving the efficiency and responsiveness of customer service. Machine learning algorithms can analyze customer data to predict future buying behavior and tailor marketing campaigns. Additionally, AI can optimize supply chain operations by forecasting demand and managing inventory levels, ensuring that products are available when and where customers want them. By harnessing the power of AI, retailers can streamline operations and deliver more personalized and efficient experiences.

The integration of online and offline channels is also evident in the rise of click-and-collect services, which allow customers to order products online and pick them up in-store. This model combines the convenience of online shopping with the immediacy of in-store pickup, offering a flexible and efficient solution for customers. Click-and-collect services have gained popularity due to their ability to save time and eliminate shipping costs. Retailers benefit from increased foot traffic to their physical stores, providing opportunities for additional sales and engagement. To enhance the click-and-collect experience, retailers are investing in technologies such as automated lockers and curbside pickup, streamlining the process and making it even more convenient for customers.

Mobile technology is another critical enabler of the future of retail. With the widespread adoption of smartphones, mobile apps have become an essential tool for engaging with customers and facilitating transactions. Mobile apps offer features such as personalized recommendations, loyalty programs, and mobile payments, creating a convenient and customized shopping experience. Retailers can also use mobile apps to send targeted promotions and notifications, driving traffic and sales. Additionally, mobile apps can integrate with in-store technologies such as beacons and QR codes, providing customers with real-time information and enhancing the shopping experience. By leveraging mobile technology, retailers can reach customers anytime and anywhere, making shopping more accessible and engaging.

The integration of online and offline retail is further supported by advancements in logistics and fulfillment. As customer expectations for fast and reliable delivery continue to rise, retailers must optimize their supply chain operations to meet these demands. Technologies such as robotics, automation, and data analytics are transforming warehousing and distribution, enabling faster and more efficient order fulfillment. For example, automated warehouses use robots to pick and pack orders, reducing labor costs and increasing speed. Data analytics can optimize routing and delivery schedules, ensuring timely and cost-effective deliveries. By investing in advanced logistics solutions, retailers can enhance their ability to fulfill orders quickly and accurately, improving customer satisfaction.

The future of retail also emphasizes the importance of experiential retail, where the focus is on creating memorable and engaging experiences for customers. Physical stores are evolving from purely transactional spaces to destinations that offer entertainment, education, and social interaction. Retailers are designing stores that incorporate elements such as interactive displays, workshops, and events, creating a dynamic and immersive environment. For example, outdoor retailer REI offers in-store classes and events related to outdoor activities, fostering a sense of community and providing added value to customers. By offering unique and engaging experiences, retailers can differentiate themselves from online competitors and build stronger connections with customers.

Sustainability is another critical factor shaping the future of retail.

As consumers become increasingly aware of environmental issues, they are demanding more sustainable practices from retailers. This includes reducing waste, using eco-friendly materials, and promoting ethical sourcing. Retailers are responding by implementing sustainable initiatives such as zero-waste packaging, carbon-neutral shipping, and recycling programs. Additionally, technology plays a role in supporting sustainability efforts. For instance, AI can optimize supply chain operations to reduce waste and emissions, while blockchain can provide transparency and traceability in sourcing and production. By prioritizing sustainability, retailers can meet consumer expectations and contribute to a more sustainable future.

The future of retail also involves reimagining the role of physical stores in a digital-first world. While e-commerce continues to grow, physical stores remain an essential part of the retail ecosystem. However, their function is evolving to complement and enhance online shopping. Physical stores are becoming hubs for experiential retail, fulfillment, and customer service. For example, stores can serve as showrooms where customers can see and try products before purchasing them online. They can also act as fulfillment centers for click-and-collect orders and same-day deliveries. By rethinking the role of physical stores, retailers can create a more integrated and flexible retail experience.

The convergence of online and offline retail also highlights the importance of customer loyalty and engagement. In a competitive marketplace, building and maintaining customer loyalty is crucial for long-term success. Retailers are using technology to create personalized and rewarding loyalty programs that incentivize repeat purchases and foster brand loyalty. For example, loyalty programs can offer personalized discounts, early access to sales, and exclusive rewards based on customer preferences and purchase history. Mobile apps and digital platforms enable retailers to engage with customers continuously, providing value beyond the transaction. By focusing on loyalty and engagement, retailers can build lasting relationships with customers and drive sustained growth.

The future of retail is characterized by the seamless integration of online and offline worlds, driven by technology and changing consumer behaviors. Omnichannel strategies, augmented reality, artificial intelligence, click-and-collect services, mobile technology, advanced logistics, experiential retail, and sustainability are all key components of this transformation. By leveraging these elements, retailers can create personalized, convenient, and immersive shopping experiences that meet the diverse needs and preferences of modern consumers. As the retail landscape continues to evolve, the ability to blend online and offline channels effectively will be critical for success. Retailers that embrace this convergence and invest in innovation will be well-positioned to thrive in the future of retail, delivering exceptional value to customers and staying ahead of the competition.

ppp

"Health tech advancements are transforming healthcare delivery. Telemedicine, AI, and wearable devices offer new ways to enhance patient care. Embrace these innovations to create a more efficient and effective healthcare system."

# EIGHTEEN

## SOCIAL MEDIA MARKETING - LEVERAGING PLATFORMS FOR BRAND GROWTH

Social media marketing has become an essential strategy for businesses aiming to achieve brand growth and customer engagement in the digital age. With billions of active users across platforms like Facebook, Instagram, Twitter, LinkedIn, TikTok, and Pinterest, social media provides a unique opportunity to connect with a global audience, build brand awareness, and drive sales. Leveraging these platforms effectively requires a comprehensive understanding of their dynamics, strategic content creation, and data-driven decision-making.

One of the primary advantages of social media marketing is its ability to reach a vast and diverse audience. Unlike traditional advertising channels, which often have limited reach and are geographically constrained, social media platforms connect businesses with users worldwide. This global reach allows brands to expand their audience and tap into new markets, enhancing their visibility and potential customer base. Additionally, social media platforms offer sophisticated targeting options, enabling businesses to reach specific demographics, interests, and behaviors, ensuring that marketing efforts are directed toward the most relevant audience segments.

Building a strong brand presence on social media begins with creating a cohesive and compelling brand identity. Consistency in visual aesthetics, messaging, and tone is crucial for establishing brand recognition and trust. This involves using consistent logos, color schemes, fonts, and imagery that reflect the brand's values and personality. A well-defined brand identity helps differentiate a business from competitors and creates a memorable impression in the minds of consumers. For instance, brands like Nike and Apple are instantly recognizable on social media due to their distinctive and consistent branding.

Content creation is at the heart of social media marketing. Engaging and high-quality content is essential for capturing the attention of users and encouraging interaction. This content can take various forms, including images, videos, infographics, articles, and user-generated content. The key is to create content that resonates with the target audience, provides value, and aligns with the brand's goals. For example, educational content can establish a brand as an authority in its industry, while entertaining content can increase engagement and shareability. Brands should also leverage storytelling to create emotional connections with their audience, making the content more relatable and impactful.

Video content, in particular, has become increasingly important in social media marketing. Platforms like YouTube, Instagram, and TikTok have popularized short-form video content, which is highly engaging and easily consumable. Videos allow brands to showcase products, share behind-the-scenes glimpses, tell stories, and engage with their audience in a dynamic way. Live streaming is another powerful tool, enabling real-time interaction and fostering a sense of community. For example, brands can host live Q&A sessions, product launches, or virtual events to connect with their audience directly and create a more immersive experience.

User-generated content (UGC) is another valuable asset in social media marketing. UGC includes any content created by users that features or mentions a brand, such as reviews, testimonials, photos, and videos. Encouraging and leveraging UGC can build trust and authenticity, as consumers tend to trust content created by their peers more than traditional advertising. Brands can incentivize UGC by running contests, featuring user content on their official channels, and engaging with users who create content. This not only increases engagement but also creates a sense of community and loyalty among customers.

Influencer marketing is a popular and effective strategy within social media marketing. Influencers are individuals with a significant following and influence within a specific niche or industry. Partnering with influencers allows brands to reach their target audience through trusted voices, enhancing credibility and expanding reach. Influencers can create authentic and relatable content that resonates with their followers, driving brand awareness and conversions. Selecting the right influencers is crucial, as their values, style, and audience should align with the brand's goals and target market. Successful influencer collaborations can lead to increased engagement, higher brand visibility, and improved customer trust.

Data analytics and insights are fundamental to effective social media marketing. Social media platforms provide a wealth of data on user behavior, engagement, and demographics. Analyzing this data helps businesses understand what content resonates with their audience, the best times to post, and the overall effectiveness of their campaigns. Key performance indicators (KPIs) such as reach, impressions, engagement rate, click-through rate, and conversion rate provide valuable insights into the performance of social media efforts. By continuously monitoring and analyzing these metrics, brands can make data-driven decisions, optimize their strategies, and achieve better results.

Engagement is a critical aspect of social media marketing. It's not enough to simply post content; brands must actively engage with their audience to build relationships and foster loyalty. This involves responding to comments, messages, and mentions promptly and authentically. Social media platforms are inherently social, and two-way communication is essential for creating a positive brand image. Engaging with users shows that the brand values their input and cares about their experiences. It also provides opportunities to address customer concerns, gather feedback, and turn negative experiences into positive ones.

Paid advertising on social media is another powerful tool for brand growth. Social media platforms offer various ad formats, including image ads, video ads, carousel ads, and sponsored posts, allowing brands to promote their content and reach a broader audience. Paid social media campaigns can be highly targeted, ensuring that ads are shown to users who are most likely to be interested in the brand. This precision targeting, combined with the ability to track and measure ad performance, makes social media advertising an effective and efficient way to drive traffic, generate leads, and boost sales. Retargeting ads, which target users who have previously interacted with the brand, can further enhance conversion rates by reminding potential customers of their interest.

Social media marketing also involves strategic planning and content scheduling. Consistency is key to maintaining an active and engaging social media presence. Brands should develop a content calendar that outlines what content will be posted, when, and on which platforms. This helps ensure a steady flow of content, aligned with marketing goals and seasonal trends. Scheduling tools such as Hootsuite, Buffer, and Sprout Social allow brands to plan and automate their posts, saving time and ensuring consistency. Additionally, these tools provide analytics and reporting features, helping brands track performance and optimize their strategies.

Storytelling is a powerful technique in social media marketing, allowing brands to create emotional connections with their audience. By sharing stories that resonate with users, brands can humanize their image and make their content more relatable. Stories can highlight the brand's mission, values, and the people behind the products. They can also showcase customer experiences, success stories, and community involvement. Platforms like Instagram and Facebook Stories provide an excellent format for storytelling, offering features such as polls, questions, and interactive stickers to engage the audience.

Social media marketing must also adapt to the evolving landscape and emerging trends. New platforms and features are continually being introduced, offering fresh opportunities for brands to connect with their audience. For instance, the rise of TikTok has introduced a new format of short, creative videos that brands can leverage to reach younger audiences. Staying updated with the latest trends and experimenting with new formats is essential for keeping the social media strategy relevant and engaging. Brands that are agile and willing to innovate are more likely to capture the attention of their audience and stay ahead of the competition.

Building a community is a long-term goal of social media marketing. A loyal and engaged community can become brand advocates, spreading positive word-of-mouth and attracting new customers. Brands can foster a sense of community by creating spaces for interaction, such as Facebook Groups, Twitter Chats, or dedicated hashtags. These spaces allow users to connect with the brand and with each other, sharing experiences, asking questions, and offering support. Hosting events, webinars, and live sessions can also strengthen community ties and provide valuable opportunities for direct engagement.

While social media marketing offers numerous benefits, it also comes with challenges. Managing multiple platforms, creating consistent and high-quality content, and keeping up with the fast-paced nature of social media can be demanding. Brands must allocate sufficient resources, including time, budget, and skilled personnel, to manage their social media efforts effectively. Additionally, the public and transparent nature of social media means that brands must be prepared to handle negative feedback and crises. Developing a crisis management plan and maintaining a proactive approach to reputation management are essential for navigating the challenges of social media marketing.

Ethics and transparency are crucial in social media marketing. Brands must ensure that their marketing practices are honest and transparent, particularly when it comes to sponsored content and influencer partnerships. Disclosing paid relationships and clearly differentiating between organic and paid content are important for maintaining trust with the audience. Authenticity should be a guiding principle, as consumers are increasingly skeptical of overly polished and insincere content. By being genuine and transparent, brands can build credibility and foster long-term relationships with their audience.

The future of social media marketing is likely to be shaped by continued advancements in technology and changing consumer behaviors. Artificial intelligence and machine learning will play a greater role in content creation, personalization, and customer service. Augmented reality and virtual reality will offer new ways for brands to create immersive and interactive experiences. Social commerce, where social media platforms integrate e-commerce features, will continue to grow, making it easier for users to discover and purchase products directly within the apps. As social media evolves, brands must stay adaptable and innovative, leveraging new technologies and trends to enhance their marketing efforts.

In conclusion, social media marketing is a powerful and multifaceted strategy for brand growth. By leveraging the unique features and vast reach of social media platforms, brands can build awareness, engage with their audience, and drive conversions. Success in social media marketing requires a strategic approach, high-quality content, active engagement, and data-driven decision-making. As technology and consumer behaviors continue to evolve, brands must remain agile and innovative, continually refining their strategies to stay relevant and effective. The potential of social media marketing is immense, offering endless opportunities for brands to connect with their audience and achieve sustained growth in the digital age.

ᑄᑄᑄ

*"The sharing economy promotes collaborative consumption and resource efficiency. Platforms like Airbnb and Uber are changing how we access goods and services. Embrace the sharing economy while ensuring fairness and sustainability."*

# NINETEEN

# The Ethics of Innovation - Balancing Progress with Responsibility

The ethics of innovation is a critical discourse that examines the intersection of technological advancement and moral responsibility. As innovation drives progress in society, it simultaneously presents ethical challenges that must be navigated to ensure that technological developments benefit humanity without causing harm. Balancing progress with responsibility requires a comprehensive understanding of the ethical implications of innovation, an adherence to ethical principles, and the establishment of frameworks that guide responsible innovation practices.

Technological innovation has the potential to solve some of the most pressing challenges faced by humanity, from healthcare and education to environmental sustainability and economic development. Advances in medical technology, for instance, have led to the development of life-saving treatments and diagnostic tools, improving health outcomes and increasing life expectancy. Similarly, innovations in renewable energy technologies are critical in addressing climate change by reducing greenhouse gas emissions and promoting sustainable energy sources. However, alongside these benefits, innovation often brings unintended consequences and ethical dilemmas that must be carefully considered.

One of the fundamental ethical concerns in innovation is the issue of equity and access. Technological advancements often create disparities in access to new technologies, exacerbating existing inequalities. For example, while digital technologies have revolutionized communication, education, and commerce, there is a persistent digital divide that leaves marginalized communities without access to these benefits. This divide can be due to factors such as socioeconomic status, geographic location, and lack of infrastructure. Ensuring equitable access to new technologies is crucial for fostering inclusive progress and preventing the deepening of social and economic inequalities.

The ethical principle of beneficence, which emphasizes actions that promote the well-being of individuals and society, is central to responsible innovation. Innovators must consider the potential benefits and harms of their creations, striving to maximize positive impacts while minimizing negative ones. This involves conducting thorough risk assessments and considering long-term consequences. For example, the development of autonomous vehicles promises to enhance transportation safety and efficiency. However, it also raises ethical questions about job displacement for drivers, the potential for accidents involving AI decision-making, and the implications for data privacy. Balancing the benefits and risks requires a careful and nuanced approach that prioritizes the well-being of all stakeholders.

Privacy is another critical ethical concern in the age of innovation, particularly with the proliferation of data-driven technologies. Big data, artificial intelligence, and the Internet of Things (IoT) generate vast amounts of personal information, raising significant privacy issues. The collection, storage, and use of this data must be governed by ethical principles that respect individuals' rights to privacy and autonomy. Unauthorized data breaches, misuse of personal information, and lack of transparency in data practices can lead to significant harm and erode public trust. Establishing robust data protection measures, obtaining informed consent, and ensuring transparency in data practices are essential for maintaining ethical standards in innovation.

The principle of non-maleficence, which emphasizes avoiding harm, is also crucial in the context of innovation. Technological advancements can have unintended harmful consequences, either due to unforeseen risks or malicious use. For instance, genetic editing technologies such as CRISPR have the potential to eradicate genetic disorders but also raise concerns about unintended genetic mutations, ethical implications of gene editing in humans, and potential misuse for eugenics. Similarly, cybersecurity threats pose significant risks to individuals, organizations, and national security, as malicious actors exploit vulnerabilities in technological systems. Innovators must proactively address these risks, implementing safeguards and ethical guidelines to prevent harm.

Transparency and accountability are fundamental to the ethics of innovation. Innovators and organizations must be transparent about their processes, goals, and the potential impacts of their technologies. This transparency fosters trust and allows stakeholders to make informed decisions about the adoption and use of new technologies. Accountability ensures that innovators are held responsible for the consequences of their actions, including addressing any negative impacts that arise. This can involve regulatory oversight, ethical review boards, and mechanisms for redress and compensation in cases of harm.

Ethical considerations in innovation also extend to the environmental impact of new technologies. Sustainable innovation practices are essential to address the environmental challenges posed by technological development. This includes considering the lifecycle of products, from resource extraction and manufacturing to disposal and recycling. For example, the production and disposal of electronic devices contribute to environmental degradation and electronic waste. Innovators must seek to develop sustainable technologies that minimize environmental harm, such as designing products for durability, reparability, and recyclability, and utilizing renewable resources and energy-efficient processes.

The rapid pace of innovation often outstrips the development of regulatory frameworks, creating a gap between technological capabilities and the ability to govern them effectively. This regulatory lag can lead to ethical issues, as new technologies may be deployed without adequate oversight or consideration of their societal impacts. Policymakers and regulators must work closely with innovators to develop agile and adaptive regulatory frameworks that keep pace with technological advancements while protecting public interest. This collaborative approach can ensure that innovation progresses responsibly, with appropriate safeguards and ethical guidelines in place.

Ethical innovation also requires a multidisciplinary perspective, incorporating insights from various fields such as ethics, sociology, law, and economics. This holistic approach ensures that the ethical implications of new technologies are thoroughly examined from multiple angles. Engaging diverse stakeholders, including affected communities, experts, and the general public, in the innovation process is crucial for understanding different perspectives and values. This inclusive approach can help identify potential ethical issues early on and develop solutions that reflect the needs and concerns of all stakeholders.

Education and awareness are vital components of fostering an ethical culture in innovation. Innovators, engineers, designers, and entrepreneurs must be equipped with the knowledge and skills to navigate ethical dilemmas and make responsible decisions. Integrating ethics education into STEM (science, technology, engineering, and mathematics) curricula can prepare future innovators to consider the broader societal impacts of their work. Additionally, ongoing professional development and training in ethical practices can help current practitioners stay informed about emerging ethical challenges and best practices.

Public engagement and dialogue are essential for ensuring that innovation aligns with societal values and expectations. Open and transparent communication about new technologies, their potential benefits, and risks can foster public trust and acceptance. Engaging the public in discussions about the ethical implications of innovation can also provide valuable insights and feedback, helping to shape responsible innovation practices. Public participation in decision-making processes, such as through public consultations and citizen assemblies, can ensure that diverse voices are heard and considered.

Ethical frameworks and principles must evolve alongside technological advancements to remain relevant and effective. Emerging technologies such as artificial intelligence, biotechnology, and quantum computing present novel ethical challenges that require continuous reflection and adaptation of ethical guidelines. For example, the development of AI raises questions about algorithmic bias, decision-making transparency, and the ethical use of autonomous systems. Biotechnology, particularly genetic editing and synthetic biology, poses ethical dilemmas related to human enhancement, biodiversity, and the potential for unintended ecological consequences. Quantum computing, with its potential to revolutionize cryptography and data security, raises concerns about privacy and the potential misuse of powerful computational capabilities.

International cooperation and collaboration are also essential for addressing the global ethical implications of innovation. Technological advancements do not respect national boundaries, and their impacts can be felt worldwide. International agreements, standards, and frameworks can provide a basis for harmonizing ethical guidelines and regulatory approaches, ensuring that innovation progresses responsibly on a global scale. Organizations such as the United Nations, the World Health Organization, and the International Telecommunication Union play a crucial role in facilitating international dialogue and cooperation on ethical issues related to innovation.

Corporate social responsibility (CSR) is a key aspect of ethical innovation, as businesses play a significant role in driving technological development. Companies must integrate ethical considerations into their business strategies, operations, and product development processes. This includes conducting ethical impact assessments, engaging with stakeholders, and adopting sustainable practices. By prioritizing ethical innovation, companies can build trust with consumers, investors, and the broader community, enhancing their reputation and long-term success.

Ultimately, the ethics of innovation is about ensuring that technological progress aligns with the values and well-being of society. It requires a commitment to ethical principles, a proactive approach to addressing potential harms, and a collaborative effort to develop responsible innovation practices. By balancing progress with responsibility, we can harness the transformative power of innovation to create a better future for all. This involves continuous reflection, dialogue, and action to navigate the complex ethical landscape of technological advancement, ensuring that innovation benefits humanity while upholding the highest ethical standards.

ᗡᗡᗡ

*"The intersection of technology, ethics, and sustainability defines the future of business. Companies must navigate these elements with care and foresight. A responsible approach will drive long-term success and societal benefit."*

# TWENTY

## CORPORATE SOCIAL RESPONSIBILITY - BUSINESSES GIVING BACK

Corporate Social Responsibility (CSR) has evolved from a peripheral concern to a central component of modern business strategy. It encompasses a broad range of practices through which businesses seek to contribute positively to society while also pursuing economic goals. CSR reflects the growing recognition that businesses have a responsibility not just to their shareholders, but also to a broader set of stakeholders, including employees, customers, communities, and the environment. By integrating social, environmental, and ethical considerations into their operations, businesses can create value that extends beyond profit, fostering sustainable development and enhancing their long-term success.

The foundation of CSR lies in the concept of the triple bottom line, which emphasizes the importance of balancing economic performance with social and environmental responsibilities. This approach challenges the traditional notion that a business's primary obligation is to maximize shareholder value, advocating instead for a more holistic view of success. By addressing the needs and interests of all stakeholders, businesses can build stronger relationships, enhance their reputation, and create a more resilient foundation for growth.

One of the most significant aspects of CSR is its focus on environmental sustainability. As concerns about climate change, resource depletion, and pollution intensify, businesses are increasingly recognizing the importance of minimizing their environmental footprint. This involves adopting sustainable practices across various aspects of their operations, such as energy use, waste management, and supply chain management. Companies are investing in renewable energy sources, improving energy efficiency, and reducing greenhouse gas emissions. For example, tech giants like Google and Apple have committed to powering their operations entirely with renewable energy, demonstrating leadership in corporate sustainability.

Sustainable supply chain management is another critical component of environmental CSR. Companies are taking steps to ensure that their suppliers adhere to environmental standards and practices, reducing the overall impact of their products. This includes sourcing materials responsibly, minimizing waste, and promoting circular economy principles, where products are designed for longevity, reuse, and recycling. By fostering sustainable supply chains, businesses can reduce their environmental impact while also enhancing the resilience and efficiency of their operations.

Social responsibility is another key dimension of CSR, encompassing a wide range of initiatives aimed at improving the well-being of employees, customers, and communities. For employees, this involves creating a positive and inclusive workplace culture, offering fair wages and benefits, and providing opportunities for professional development. Companies that prioritize employee well-being often see benefits such as increased productivity, higher job satisfaction, and reduced turnover. For example, companies like Salesforce and Patagonia are known for their strong commitment to employee welfare, offering extensive benefits, flexible work arrangements, and opportunities for growth.

Customer-focused CSR initiatives aim to build trust and loyalty by addressing consumer concerns and enhancing the overall customer experience. This can include ensuring product safety and quality, promoting ethical marketing practices, and engaging in transparent communication. Companies are also increasingly responding to consumer demand for ethical and sustainable products, developing offerings that align with these values. For example, brands like TOMS and Warby Parker have built their business models around social impact, with initiatives such as donating a pair of shoes or glasses for every pair sold.

Community engagement and philanthropy are central to CSR, as businesses seek to give back to the communities in which they operate. This can take many forms, including charitable donations, volunteer programs, and partnerships with non-profit organizations. By supporting local initiatives and addressing social issues, companies can strengthen their ties with the community and contribute to social cohesion and development. For instance, companies like Microsoft and Starbucks have robust community engagement programs, supporting education, health, and social services in the communities where they operate.

Ethical governance and transparency are fundamental to effective CSR. Businesses must adhere to high ethical standards in their operations, ensuring that they act with integrity and accountability. This includes complying with laws and regulations, avoiding corruption and unethical practices, and fostering a culture of transparency. Companies that prioritize ethical governance build trust with stakeholders and reduce the risk of reputational damage and legal issues. For example, companies like Johnson & Johnson and Unilever have been recognized for their commitment to ethical governance, implementing robust compliance programs and promoting transparency in their operations.

CSR also involves addressing broader societal challenges, such as poverty, inequality, and access to education and healthcare. Companies can leverage their resources and expertise to make a meaningful impact in these areas, contributing to the achievement of global development goals. For example, pharmaceutical companies like Merck and GlaxoSmithKline have initiatives aimed at improving access to essential medicines in low-income countries, addressing global health challenges. Similarly, technology companies are working to bridge the digital divide by providing access to technology and digital literacy programs in underserved communities.

The integration of CSR into business strategy requires a comprehensive approach that involves all levels of the organization. This includes setting clear goals and objectives, developing policies and practices that align with CSR principles, and measuring and reporting on progress. Effective CSR requires strong leadership and a commitment to continuous improvement, as well as collaboration with stakeholders to understand their needs and expectations.

Measuring the impact of CSR initiatives is crucial for demonstrating their value and effectiveness. Companies use various metrics and frameworks to assess their performance, such as the Global Reporting Initiative (GRI) standards, the United Nations Sustainable Development Goals (SDGs), and the Carbon Disclosure Project (CDP). By tracking and reporting on their CSR activities, businesses can identify areas for improvement, enhance transparency, and communicate their achievements to stakeholders.

The benefits of CSR extend beyond social and environmental impact, offering significant business advantages. Companies that embrace CSR often see enhanced brand reputation and customer loyalty, as consumers increasingly prefer to support businesses that align with their values. CSR can also drive innovation, as companies develop new products and services that address social and environmental challenges. Additionally, CSR can improve employee engagement and attract top talent, as individuals seek to work for organizations that have a positive impact on society.

The evolving landscape of CSR is shaped by emerging trends and challenges. One such trend is the increasing importance of stakeholder engagement, as companies recognize the value of involving stakeholders in their CSR efforts. This includes engaging with employees, customers, communities, investors, and other stakeholders to understand their perspectives and collaborate on solutions. Effective stakeholder engagement can enhance the relevance and impact of CSR initiatives, fostering stronger relationships and trust.

Another emerging trend is the integration of CSR with corporate purpose and values. Companies are increasingly aligning their CSR efforts with their core mission and values, creating a more cohesive and authentic approach to social responsibility. This involves embedding CSR into the company's culture and decision-making processes, ensuring that it is a fundamental aspect of how the business operates. For example, companies like Ben & Jerry's and The Body Shop have built their brands around a strong sense of purpose, integrating social and environmental responsibility into their business models.

The role of technology in CSR is also expanding, offering new opportunities for innovation and impact. Digital technologies, such as artificial intelligence, blockchain, and data analytics, can enhance the effectiveness of CSR initiatives by providing new tools for transparency, efficiency, and stakeholder engagement. For example, blockchain technology can be used to track and verify the sustainability of supply chains, ensuring that products are sourced ethically. Data analytics can provide insights into social and environmental impacts, helping companies make informed decisions and measure progress.

Climate change remains one of the most pressing challenges for CSR, as businesses must address the urgent need for environmental sustainability. Companies are increasingly committing to ambitious climate goals, such as achieving net-zero emissions and transitioning to renewable energy. This requires innovative solutions and collaboration across industries and sectors. For instance, the Science Based Targets initiative provides a framework for companies to set and achieve climate goals that align with the latest climate science.

The COVID-19 pandemic has highlighted the importance of CSR, as businesses play a critical role in supporting their employees, customers, and communities during times of crisis. Companies have responded by providing financial support, health and safety measures, and innovative solutions to address the challenges posed by the pandemic. The crisis has underscored the need for resilience and adaptability in CSR, as businesses navigate an uncertain and rapidly changing landscape.

In conclusion, Corporate Social Responsibility is a multifaceted and evolving concept that encompasses a wide range of practices aimed at creating positive social, environmental, and economic impact. By integrating CSR into their operations, businesses can contribute to sustainable development, build stronger relationships with stakeholders, and enhance their long-term success. The future of CSR is shaped by emerging trends, technological advancements, and the ongoing need to address global challenges. As businesses continue to navigate this landscape, a commitment to ethical principles, transparency, and stakeholder engagement will be essential for driving meaningful and lasting change. Through CSR, businesses have the opportunity to not only give back to society but also to create a better, more sustainable future for all.

ƊƊƊ

"Innovation is a journey of continuous learning
and adaptation. Embrace the unknown with
curiosity and courage. The future belongs to those
who innovate responsibly and lead with purpose."

# TWENTY-ONE
## SUMMARY

The landscape of modern business is being shaped by a confluence of transformative trends and technologies, each carrying significant implications for how organizations operate, engage with stakeholders, and drive sustainable growth. From the integration of digital technologies and the rise of artificial intelligence to the ethical considerations of innovation and the imperative of corporate social responsibility, businesses today are navigating a complex environment that demands agility, responsibility, and a forward-thinking mindset.

Digital transformation is at the forefront of this evolution, reshaping industries by integrating technology into all areas of business operations. This involves leveraging tools such as cloud computing, big data analytics, and the Internet of Things (IoT) to improve efficiency, enhance customer experiences, and drive innovation. Businesses that successfully embrace digital transformation can gain a competitive edge by streamlining processes, reducing costs, and creating new value propositions. However, this transformation also necessitates a focus on cybersecurity to protect digital assets and ensure the privacy and security of sensitive information. As cyber threats become more sophisticated, robust security measures and a proactive approach to managing risks are essential.

Artificial intelligence (AI) and machine learning (ML) are revolutionizing business intelligence and decision-making. These technologies enable organizations to analyze vast amounts of data, uncover patterns, and make predictive and prescriptive decisions that enhance efficiency and effectiveness. In sectors such as healthcare, finance, and retail, AI-driven insights are optimizing operations, improving customer experiences, and driving innovation. However, the deployment of AI and ML also raises ethical concerns, including issues of bias, transparency, and accountability. Ensuring that AI systems are fair, transparent, and used responsibly is crucial for maintaining trust and maximizing their benefits.

Blockchain technology extends beyond its origins in cryptocurrency to offer transformative potential across various industries. By providing a decentralized and secure method for recording transactions and managing data, blockchain enhances transparency, security, and efficiency. Applications range from supply chain management and financial services to healthcare and voting systems. Blockchain's ability to create immutable records and facilitate trust in digital interactions makes it a powerful tool for addressing challenges related to data integrity and security. However, the widespread adoption of blockchain requires overcoming technical, regulatory, and scalability challenges.

The gig economy is redefining the workforce landscape by offering flexible work arrangements that cater to diverse lifestyles and preferences. Platforms such as Uber, Lyft, and TaskRabbit connect gig workers with short-term employment opportunities, providing convenience and autonomy. While the gig economy offers benefits such as flexibility and additional income streams, it also raises concerns about job security, benefits, and workers' rights. Balancing the advantages of gig work with the need for fair labor practices and protections is essential for creating a sustainable and equitable workforce.

Remote work has undergone a significant transformation, accelerated by the COVID-19 pandemic. Advances in communication and collaboration technologies have enabled businesses to maintain productivity and continuity despite physical distance. Remote work offers benefits such as increased flexibility, reduced commuting time, and access to a broader talent pool. However, it also presents challenges related to employee engagement, collaboration, and work-life balance. Developing effective remote work policies and fostering a supportive remote work culture are critical for maximizing the benefits and addressing the challenges of this new work paradigm.

Sustainability and green business practices are becoming central to corporate strategies as environmental concerns intensify. Businesses are adopting sustainable practices to reduce their environmental footprint, including minimizing waste, conserving resources, and transitioning to renewable energy sources. These efforts not only contribute to environmental protection but also enhance brand reputation and meet growing consumer demand for eco-friendly products. Sustainable supply chain management, circular economy principles, and green innovation are key components of a comprehensive sustainability strategy. By prioritizing sustainability, businesses can drive long-term value and contribute to global efforts to combat climate change.

E-commerce has evolved significantly, driven by changes in consumer behavior and technological advancements. Online shopping platforms offer convenience, variety, and personalized experiences, reshaping how consumers purchase goods and services. The integration of technologies such as AI, AR, and data analytics enhances the e-commerce experience by providing personalized recommendations, virtual try-ons, and efficient supply chain management. However, the growth of e-commerce also necessitates addressing challenges related to data privacy, cybersecurity, and environmental impact. Sustainable e-commerce practices, such as eco-friendly packaging and carbon-neutral shipping, are becoming increasingly important for balancing growth with responsibility.

Big data is a powerful asset that drives insights and innovation across various sectors. The ability to collect, process, and analyze vast amounts of data enables businesses to make informed decisions, optimize operations, and personalize customer experiences. Big data analytics is used in marketing to understand consumer behavior, in healthcare to improve patient outcomes, and in finance to detect fraud and assess risk. However, the ethical use of big data requires addressing privacy concerns, ensuring data security, and avoiding biases that can lead to discriminatory outcomes. Transparent and responsible data practices are essential for maintaining trust and maximizing the benefits of big data.

Personalization and customer experience are critical factors in building brand loyalty and driving business success. Advances in technology enable businesses to deliver tailored experiences that meet individual customer needs and preferences. Personalization can be achieved through data-driven insights, AI-powered recommendations, and interactive digital platforms. Enhancing the customer experience involves creating seamless and engaging interactions across all touchpoints, from online shopping to customer service. By prioritizing personalization and customer experience, businesses can differentiate themselves in a competitive market and foster long-term relationships with their customers.

Virtual and augmented reality (VR and AR) are enhancing user experiences by creating immersive and interactive digital environments. VR provides fully immersive experiences by transporting users to computer-generated worlds, while AR overlays digital information onto the physical world. These technologies have applications in entertainment, education, healthcare, and retail. For example, VR can simulate real-world scenarios for training and education, while AR can enhance shopping experiences by allowing customers to visualize products in their environment. The development of more accessible and user-friendly VR and AR devices is driving their adoption and expanding their potential.

Social media marketing leverages the vast reach and engagement capabilities of social media platforms to build brand awareness, engage with customers, and drive sales. Effective social media marketing involves creating high-quality content, engaging with users, and leveraging data analytics to optimize strategies. Influencer marketing, user-generated content, and paid advertising are key components of a comprehensive social media strategy. By actively engaging with their audience and providing valuable content, businesses can build strong online communities and enhance their brand presence.

Corporate social responsibility (CSR) is an integral part of modern business strategy, reflecting the growing recognition that businesses have a responsibility to contribute positively to society. CSR encompasses a wide range of practices, including environmental sustainability, social responsibility, and ethical governance. Companies are adopting sustainable practices, supporting community initiatives, and ensuring ethical conduct in their operations. By integrating CSR into their business strategies, companies can enhance their reputation, build stronger stakeholder relationships, and contribute to sustainable development.

The ethics of innovation emphasize the importance of balancing technological progress with moral responsibility. As innovation drives societal advancement, it also presents ethical challenges that must be navigated to ensure that new technologies benefit humanity without causing harm. Key ethical considerations include equity and access, privacy, non-maleficence, transparency, and environmental impact. Innovators must conduct thorough risk assessments, engage with diverse stakeholders, and adhere to ethical principles to navigate the complex ethical landscape of technological advancement.

Blending online and offline retail worlds creates a seamless and integrated shopping experience for consumers. Omnichannel retailing, which combines digital and physical retail spaces, enhances customer satisfaction and loyalty by providing a consistent experience across all touchpoints. Technologies such as AR, AI, and data analytics play a crucial role in bridging the gap between online and offline retail. Click-and-collect services, mobile technology, and experiential retail are key components of this transformation. By leveraging these elements, retailers can create personalized, convenient, and immersive shopping experiences that meet the diverse needs and preferences of modern consumers.

EdTech and online learning are transforming education by providing greater accessibility, flexibility, and personalization. Digital platforms and tools enable students to learn at their own pace and access a wealth of educational resources from anywhere in the world. Adaptive learning technologies, interactive multimedia content, and virtual classrooms enhance the learning experience and improve educational outcomes. The integration of technology into education also supports lifelong learning and professional development, preparing individuals for the demands of the digital age. However, addressing challenges such as digital equity, student engagement, and data privacy is essential for maximizing the benefits of EdTech.

Health tech advances are revolutionizing healthcare delivery by improving access, efficiency, and patient outcomes. Telemedicine, wearable devices, AI, and blockchain are reshaping how healthcare services are provided and managed. These technologies enable remote consultations, continuous health monitoring, personalized treatment plans, and secure data management. By integrating health tech innovations into healthcare systems, providers can enhance the quality of care, reduce costs, and improve patient experiences. Addressing ethical considerations, such as data privacy and equitable access, is crucial for ensuring the responsible deployment of health tech.

The sharing economy promotes collaborative consumption by enabling individuals to share access to goods and services. Platforms such as Airbnb, Uber, and Rent the Runway facilitate peer-to-peer exchanges, providing flexibility and cost savings for users. The sharing economy leverages underutilized assets, reduces waste, and fosters community engagement. However, it also raises challenges related to regulation, labor rights, and data privacy. Balancing the benefits of the sharing economy with the need for fair and ethical practices is essential for creating a sustainable and equitable model of collaborative consumption.

In summary, the modern business landscape is being reshaped by a multitude of trends and technologies that offer significant opportunities for growth, innovation, and positive societal impact. From digital transformation and AI to CSR and the sharing economy, businesses are navigating a complex and dynamic environment that demands a strategic and responsible approach. By embracing these trends and addressing the associated challenges, businesses can drive sustainable growth, enhance their competitive advantage, and contribute to a better future for all stakeholders. The convergence of technological advancement, ethical responsibility, and stakeholder engagement will continue to shape the future of business, creating a more inclusive, sustainable, and resilient global economy.

ᑭᑭᑭ

# Citation And References

This book represents the culmination of extensive research and meticulous analysis, incorporating a diverse range of sources, including numerous books, scholarly studies, and personal experiences. Additionally, I have scoured various websites to gather relevant information and data essential for the compilation of this work. I have taken every precaution to ensure the accuracy of the information presented and have diligently cited all sources to acknowledge their contributions.

Despite these efforts, the possibility of inadvertent errors remains. I deeply value the insights of my readers and appreciate any feedback that can help identify and rectify such inaccuracies. I encourage you to bring any discrepancies to my attention.

Your feedback is not only welcome but crucial, as it will aid in correcting current editions and enhancing the content of future ones. I am committed to maintaining the highest standards of accuracy and reliability in my work and thank you for your support and understanding.

Additionally, I firmly uphold the principle of freedom of speech and expression as guaranteed under Article 19(1)(a) of the Constitution of India, and I respect the diverse viewpoints and expressions of all readers.

ᑭᑭᑭ

# Other Books Of The Author

1. Empowering Minds: A Journey into Women's Self-Discovery and Power
2. The Dynamics of Motivation: Catalyzing Thought into Action
3. Meditation and Mental Well Being: The Path to Inner Peace and Clarity
4. The Psychology of Child Education: Nurturing Future Generations
5. Ethical Enlightenment: A Modern Guide to Living with Integrity
6. Voices of Empowerment: Stories of Women Rising Against Odds
7. Social Psychology in Everyday Life: Understanding Human Connections
8. The Essence of Motivational Speaking: Inspiring Change in Others
9. Balancing Acts: Women, Work, and the Will to Lead
10. Guiding with Grace: Raising Children with Compassion and Awareness
11. The Power of Positive Aging: Embracing Life After Fifty
12. Building Resilient Communities: Social Work in Action
13. The Ethical Educator: Principles for Teaching and Learning
14. From Insight to Impact: Social Psychology for a Better World
15. The Ethics of Empathy: A Guide to Ethical Living
16. The Science of Empowering the Self: Navigating Life's Challenges with Psychological Wisdom
17. The Mindful Conscious Leader: Meditation Techniques for Modern Management
18. Pioneering Spirit: Women's Pathways to Leadership and Empowerment
19. Feeling to Healing: The Role of Emotional Intelligence in Child Development
20. Transformative Talks and Words of Inspiration: Insights into Motivational Oratory

21. Green Ethics: A Path to Sustainable Living
22. Spiritual Integrity: Navigating Life with Moral Compassion
23. Clean Living, Clean Society: The Ethics of Cleanliness
24. Patriotic Spirits: Building a Nation on Positive Attitudes
25. Innovative Integrity & Vibrant Visions: The Ethical and Entrepreneurial Spirit of Gujarat
26. Youthful Visions, Endless Possibilities: Inspiring Ethics and Motivation in Children
27. Living Your Legacy: How to Motivate Others by Living Your Values
28. Secret of Healing Conversations: Ethical Practices in Counselling and Therapy
29. Creative Kindness: Crafting a Life of Compassion and Creativity
30. The Power of Appreciation: How Gratitude Can Transform Your Relationships
31. Bhagavad-Gita: Messages
32. Science of Art: The New Frontier of Fashion Modernism
33. Vivekananda's Virtues: A Blueprint for Modern Living
34. Empower Her: Navigating the Path to Women's Entrepreneurship
35. The Boundless Classroom: Innovations in Global Education
36. The Language of Leadership: Communicating with Authenticity and Impact
37. The Warrior's Mantra: Deciphering the Hanuman Chalisa
38. Echoes of Empathy: Transformative Stories of Social Service
39. Artful Living: Cultivating Creativity in Your Daily Routine
40. Finding Your Why: Discovering Your Passions and Charting Your Course
41. The Role of Social Media in Shaping Self-Esteem and Interpersonal Relationships among Adolescents
42. Karma's Tapestry: Weaving a Life of Selfless Service
43. Altruistic Alchemy: Transforming Lives Through Giving
44. The Blueprint of Pro-Activeness and Productivity: Crafting Habits for Success
45. The Simplicity with Grounded Wisdom: Embracing Authenticity

in a Complex World


46. Secret of Solopreneur's Odyssey: Navigating the Path to Self-Employment

47. Exploring Tapestry of Peace: Global Perspectives on Harmony

48. The Art and Actions of Connection: Mastering Communication for Impact

49. She Governs and at the Helm: Strategies for Political Empowerment

50. Rising Above and Rising with Grace: A Woman's Roadmap to Career Mastery

51. The Effect of Networking & Connectedness: Building Strategic Alliances for Women

52. Beyond his Barriers: Women Thriving in Male-Dominated Fields

53. Secret of Inner Compass: Navigating Life with Intuition

54. Creative & Pro-Active Muses: A Celebration of Women in the Arts

55. Unburdened: The Art of Releasing the Past

56. Amplified Voices: Speeches of Women that Astonished the World

57. Secret of Manifesting Dreams: A Woman's Guide to Intentional Living

58. Ethics and Value Based Education: Reimagining Japan's School System

59. The Moral Compass Curriculum: A Holistic Approach

60. Tech with Heart: Integrating Ethics into Digital Learning

61. Honoring Virtue: Recognizing Ethical Excellence in Education

62. Raising Good Humans: A Guide to Character Development

63. The Spark Within: Nurturing Creativity in Children

64. The Teenager Whisperer: Navigating Adolescence with Grace

65. Igniting a Passion for Learning: Inspiring Lifelong Curiosity

66. The Habit Lab: Cultivating Positive Behaviors in Children

67. Seeds of Empathy: Fostering Compassion in Young Hearts

68. The Reading Revolution: Inspiring a Love of Books in Children

69. The Learning Brain: Unlocking the Secrets of Student Success

70. Teaching for All: Differentiated Instruction Strategies

71. The Time Alchemist: Mastering Time Management for Peak Performance

72. The Resilience Factor: Transforming Setbacks into Stepping Stones
73. The Healing Touch of Nature: An Introduction to Naturopathy
74. Echoes of the Past: Healing Through Past Life Regression
75. The Spiritual Healer's Handbook: Exploring Energy Medicine
76. Crystal Clarity: Unveiling the Power of Gemstones
77. The Dream Weaver's Guide: Decoding the Language of Dreams
78. Emotional Alchemy: Transforming Pain into Power
79. Sonic Serenity: Harnessing Sound for Stress Relief
80. The Entrepreneur's Playbook: Launching Your Business with Confidence
81. Productivity Unleashed: Time Management Strategies for Entrepreneurs
82. The Problem Solver's Toolkit: Creative Solutions for Business Challenges
83. The Future is Now: Emerging Trends in Business
84. The Curious Explorer: A Child's Guide to Scientific Discovery
85. Digital Pioneers: Empowering Kids in the Tech World
86. The Young Philosopher's Guide: Exploring Life's Big Questions
87. Finding Your Voice: Communication Skills for Confident Kids
88. Nature's Playground: A Child's Guide to Outdoor Adventure
89. Growing a Greener Tomorrow: A Guide to Tree Planting & Conservation
90. Driving with Purpose: Ethical Choices on the Road
91. The Healing Touch: Cultivating Compassion in Healthcare
92. Navigating the Digital Landscape: Ethics in the Age of Social Media
93. The Ethical Closet: A Guide to Sustainable Fashion
94. The Mindful Voyager: Sustainable Travel Practices
95. The Feminine Divine: Honoring the Goddesses of India
96. Sacred Sounds: Chanting Your Way to Inner Peace
97. The Yoga Path: Uniting with the Divine Within
98. Rites of Passage: Creating Meaningful Ceremonies
99. The Chakra System: A Map of Inner Transformation
100. Spiritual Sangha: Finding Community through Satsang and

Bhajan

101. Pilgrimage of the Soul: Spiritual Journeys in India

❦❦❦

# Contact

Dr. Minakshi Bansal
Social Activist
Ahmedabad, Gujarat, Bharat
minakshiindiag20@yahoo.com

❥❥❥

|| LOKAHA SAMASTHAHA SUKHINO BHAVANTU ||